Variants • Weapons • Equipment

Arado
Ar 234 A

Military Aircraft
In Detail
Variants • Weapons • Equipment

Arado
Ar 234 A

J. Richard Smith
with Hans-Georg Dachner

Acknowledgements | Special thanks must go to Hans-Georg Dachner who unselfishly gave us the results of his research on the aircraft and provided many of the drawings. The authors would also like to thank Horst Götz, Ubbo Janssen, Anthony L. Kay, Dr. Volker Koos, Rüdiger Kosin, Hans Rebeski, Günter Sengfelder and Erich Sommer.

First published 2006

ISBN (10) 1 85780 225 X
ISBN (13) 978 1 85780 225 2

Produced by Chevron Publishing Limited

Project Editors: Eddie J. Creek and Mark Nelson/Chevron Publishing

© Narrative text: Richard J.Smith
© Line artwork: Arthur Bentley, Hans-Georg Dachner and Günter Sengfelder.
© Colour Profiles: Tim Brown

Published by Midland Publishing an imprint of Ian Allan Publishing Ltd. Hersham, Surrey, KT12 4RG

Printed in England by Ian Allan Printing Ltd, Hersham, Surrey KT12 4RG

Visit the Ian Allan Publishing website at www.ianallanpublishing.com

MIDLAND

An imprint of
Ian Allan Publishing

www.ianallanpublishing.com

Contents

Arado

Arado – a name unique among major German wartime aircraft manufacturers in that it was not named after its founder or the area in which it was established.

△ During the late 1920s, Dipl.-Ing. Walter Blume took over from Walther Rethel as head of the Arado design office. He is seen here in his NSFK uniform.

The company began life as the *Flugzeugbau Friedrichshafen GmbH*, a manufacturer of important floatplanes such as the FF 49c which saw widespread service during the First World War. In November 1920 its disused factory buildings at Warnemünde on the Baltic coast were bought by the German industrialist, Hugo Stinnes, who used them to produce furniture, ice yachts and sailing boats. One of the latter, produced by the company for the South American market, was plough-like in shape. The Spanish word for plough is *'arado'*, thus the success of the boat prompted Stinnes to change the name of the company to the *Arado Handelsgesellschaft mbH* in 1925. The name was to seem doubly appropriate about a year later when the company engaged the services of a talented aircraft designer, Walter Rethel, and began building aeroplanes under licence. The German word for plough is *'pflug'* - phonetically similar to that for flight, *'flug'*.

Although early efforts were concentrated on producing aircraft under licence, Rethel's first indigenous design, the Arado S I two-seat trainer, was built in 1925. This was followed by a number of other biplane fighters and trainers and two sporting monoplanes. Hugo Stinnes died in 1924 and later Walter Blume took over from Rethel as chief designer. Early in 1933 the appointment of Hitler as German Chancellor led to the transfer of a large amount of capital to the company. It now concentrated solely on aircraft manufacture, being renamed *Arado Flugzeugwerke GmbH* on 4 March. Two important early designs produced by the new company were the Ar 66 two-seat trainer and Ar 68 single-seat fighter biplanes for the fledgling *Luftwaffe*. Most of Arado's production capacity was, however, given over to the licence-building of such aircraft as the He 59, He 60, He 111 and Bf 109. On 6 September 1934, Arado bought a former iron foundry at Neuendorf west of Brandenburg, aircraft production beginning there six months later.

The company was nationalised in 1936, an upturn in its fortunes coming with the appearance of the Ar 95 floatplane and the superb Ar 96 tandem two-seat trainer two years later. This aircraft was swiftly adopted as the standard advanced trainer for the *Luftwaffe* and over 3,000 were built. This was followed by the Ar 196, a two-seat reconnaissance and coastal patrol floatplane, which saw widespread service during the Second World War. Prototypes of two versions were completed, one

▷ The BMW IV powered Arado SC I was a two-seat advanced trainer which was used in some numbers by the DVS schools at Berlin-Staaken and later Braunschweig and Schleissheim.

◁ The Ar 95 biplane floatplane was not accepted for use by the Luftwaffe initially, Arado receiving export orders for the aircraft from both Turkey and Chile (the latter a landplane version). The Chilean machines were delivered, but those for Turkey were diverted to Germany following the outbreak of the Second World War.

with twin floats, the other with a large central float balanced by two outriggers but the former was preferred.

Despite this, most of Arado's production facilities were devoted to the licence-construction of such strategically important types as the He 111, Bf 109 and Fw 190. Almost 4,000 of the latter were built at Warnemünde, Brandenburg and a new plant at Babelsberg near Berlin by the end of 1944. The factories also undertook the production of Ju 88s and latterly the He 177 four-engined bomber.

Several fascinating aircraft prototypes did, however, emerge from Arado's own design offices during the early years of the Second World War. These included the Ar 231, a collapsible reconnaissance aircraft designed to be stowed aboard a U-boat and the Ar 233, a small amphibian transport of which the only prototype was destroyed before it could fly. More important than these were the Ar 232 (project designation E 440), a large transport capable of carrying loads such as two *Kübelwagen* scout cars and the Ar 240 (E 625) twin-engined multi-purpose aircraft with remotely-controlled defensive armament. One of the features of the former was its multi-wheel undercarriage onto which it could be lowered to facilitate loading. Two versions were produced, one powered by two large radials, the other by four smaller engines. Only about ten prototypes of the Ar 240 were built, the type having difficult handling characteristics but an excellent performance. It was used operationally by the *Luftwaffe* on reconnaissance sorties over England.

Although these designs achieved success in their specialist fields, it is undoubtedly the Ar 234 for which the company is now best remembered.

▽ Two versions of the Ar 232 were built, the A-series powered by two BMW 801 engines and the B-series with four BMW 132s (seen here). To enable loads to be easily driven aboard the aircraft, it could be lowered onto its multi-wheel undercarriage and a rear hinged door lowered.

▽ Although only a small number of Ar 240 multi-purpose aircraft were completed it was used operational in many of theatres of the war. Horst Götz, who later flew the Ar 234, flew a number of reconnaissance sorties over the British Isles in the sixth prototype coded T9+GL.

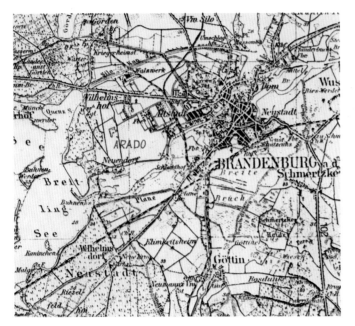

△ The Arado factory at Brandenburg

▷ This aerial photograph of Arado's Brandenburg-Neundorf factory, taken on 9 May 1944 should be compared with the map (*opposite page*).

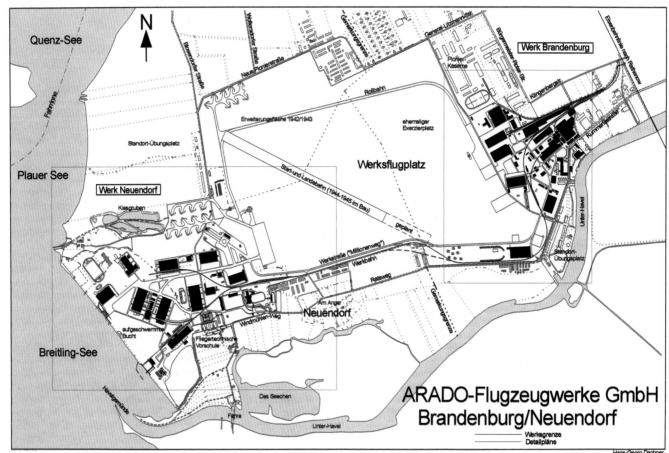

Quenz-See

Plauer See

Werk Neuendorf

Breitling-See

Werk Brandenburg

Werksflugplatz

Neuendorf

ARADO-Flugzeugwerke GmbH
Brandenburg/Neuendorf

Werksgrenze
Detailpläne

Hans-Georg Dachner

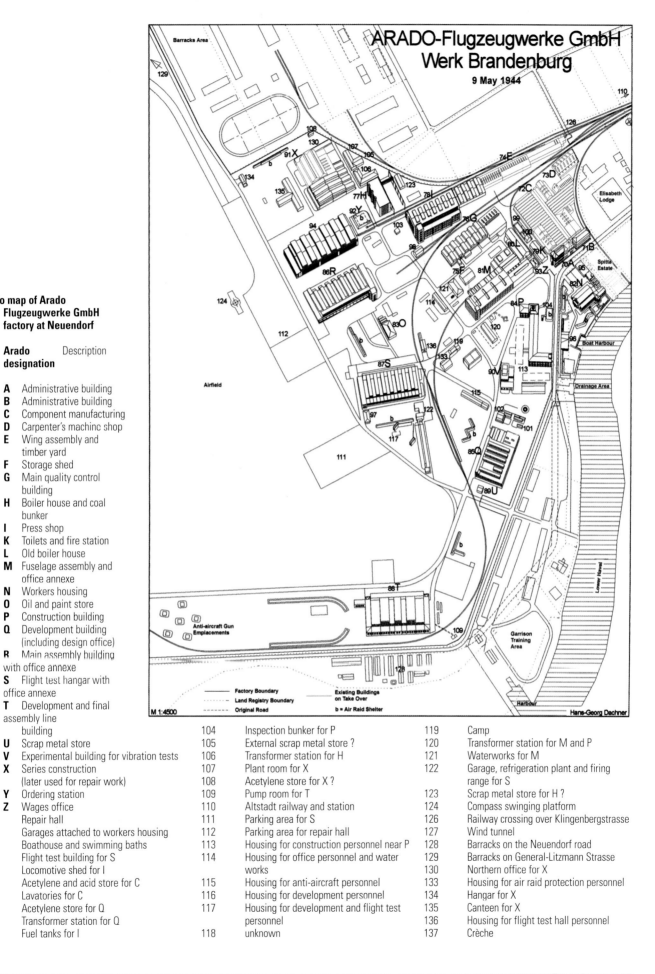

ARADO-Flugzeugwerke GmbH
Werk Brandenburg
9 May 1944

Key to map of Arado Flugzeugwerke GmbH factory at Neuendorf

Key	Arado designation	Description
70	A	Administrative building
71	B	Administrative building
72	C	Component manufacturing
73	D	Carpenter's machine shop
74	E	Wing assembly and timber yard
75	F	Storage shed
76	G	Main quality control building
77	H	Boiler house and coal bunker
78	I	Press shop
79	K	Toilets and fire station
80	L	Old boiler house
81	M	Fuselage assembly and office annexe
82	N	Workers housing
83	O	Oil and paint store
84	P	Construction building
85	Q	Development building (including design office)
86	R	Main assembly building with office annexe
87	S	Flight test hangar with office annexe
88	T	Development and final assembly line building
89	U	Scrap metal store
90	V	Experimental building for vibration tests
91	X	Series construction (later used for repair work)
92	Y	Ordering station
93	Z	Wages office
94		Repair hall
95		Garages attached to workers housing
96		Boathouse and swimming baths
97		Flight test building for S
98		Locomotive shed for I
99		Acetylene and acid store for C
100		Lavatories for C
101		Acetylene store for Q
102		Transformer station for Q
103		Fuel tanks for I

104	Inspection bunker for P
105	External scrap metal store ?
106	Transformer station for H
107	Plant room for X
108	Acetylene store for X ?
109	Pump room for T
110	Altstadt railway and station
111	Parking area for S
112	Parking area for repair hall
113	Housing for construction personnel near P
114	Housing for office personnel and water works
115	Housing for anti-aircraft personnel
116	Housing for development personnel
117	Housing for development and flight test personnel
118	unknown

119	Camp
120	Transformer station for M and P
121	Waterworks for M
122	Garage, refrigeration plant and firing range for S
123	Scrap metal store for H ?
124	Compass swinging platform
126	Railway crossing over Klingenbergstrasse
127	Wind tunnel
128	Barracks on the Neuendorf road
129	Barracks on General-Litzmann Strasse
130	Northern office for X
133	Housing for air raid protection personnel
134	Hangar for X
135	Canteen for X
136	Housing for flight test hall personnel
137	Crèche

M 1:4500

Factory Boundary
Land Registry Boundary
Original Road
Existing Buildings on Take Over
b = Air Raid Shelter

Hans-Georg Dachner

Engines

Much of the credit for the establishment of a turbojet engine development programme in Germany must go to a young graduate, Dipl.-Ing. Helmut Schelp.

After joining LC 1, the *Forschungsabteilung* (Research Department) of the RLM or German Aviation Ministry's Technical Office in August 1937, Dipl.-Ing. Helmut Schelp was placed in charge of pulse- and ramjet research, but he had already concluded that gas turbines were far more promising. His views, first put forward to the DVL [1], proved somewhat controversial as he was later to explain:

"They caused a furore, but in the end my views prevailed and I was able to define and describe a family of jet engines, including turboprops and pure turbojets. Some distinguished engineers thought my ideas were pure fantasy, and my professors and examiners were very doubtful. At this time I was working on my own and knew nothing of Heinkel, Junkers or British work in this field."

In September 1938, Dr. Adolf Baeumker, the head of LC 1, suggested to Schelp that he transfer to *Abteilung* LC 8 (responsible for aircraft engine development) where his theories might gain more support. The head of LC 8, Wolfram Eisenlohr, was initially sceptical of gas turbines, but Schelp soon found an ally in *Dipl.-Ing.* Hans Mauch, the *Referent für Sondertriebwerke* (Technical Advisor for Special Power Plants) who, up to that time, had been interested primarily in rocket engines. Schelp explained the possibilities of gas turbine engines to Mauch, and was able to convince him that it was time to initiate the wider development of such power plants.

During the autumn of 1938, the two men visited the four main aircraft engine manufacturers, Daimler-Benz, Junkers, BMW and Bramo *(Brandenburgische Motorenwerke GmbH)* but only achieved limited success in persuading these companies to take up the development of gas turbine engines. Daimler-Benz showed little interest until sometime later, but the other three did embark on some form of turbojet development.

JUNKERS

As early as 1936, the Junkers aircraft company, as distinct from the engine department, had begun work on gas turbine development under Professor *Dr.-Ing.* Herbert Wagner. Although only 35 years old, Wagner was recognized as one of the most brilliant and progressive aeronautical minds in Germany. It was hoped that he would be able "...to bring new life and new ideas into the somewhat inflexible field of aircraft construction". Wagner's work began as a study for a high-altitude aircraft with a pressurized cabin. During this research he became involved in a study for a large, long-range, high-altitude aircraft, capable of trans-Atlantic flight. He quickly reached the conclusion that no conventional aero-engine would be suitable to propel such an aeroplane and soon gained permission to research into new forms of aircraft propulsion.

At the same time, Professor Otto Mader of the Junkers engine company was also working on turbojet development,

△ Professor Otto Mader of the Junkers engine works was rather conservative in his views on the development of the turbojet engine, feeling that they would only divert resources from the further development of piston engines.

1. *Deutsche Versuchsanstalt für Luftfahrt* (German Experimental Institution for Aviation).

although many considered his ideas far too conservative. The situation was remedied by the arrival of *Dipl.-Ing.* Anselm Franz, a 36-year old graduate from Graz Technical High School. In August 1938 he was asked to undertake a general survey of all gas turbines within the company. This resulted in his rejection of the earlier work undertaken by Herbert Wagner and his assistant Max Adolf Müller and a conviction that the only way to obtain the performance required would be to use a simple turbojet configuration.

Franz later explained: "In 1939 the RLM wanted us to take over Wagner's engine, but I refused and during the autumn of that year we received a government contract for our own T 1, later to become known as the Jumo 004 A. This can claim to be the world's first successful axial flow turbojet, a configuration that became the standard for jet engine design. The Jumo 004 was also the first jet engine in volume production and combat service." In Franz's view, Wagner was: "... a very aggressive person, attempting to go, as Mader saw it, beyond what was then possible. He was a brilliant man, but he did not have a feel for the realities." In retrospect, it is obvious that Wagner had allowed Müller to spread his very limited manpower over too many divergent projects. It would have been better if he had concentrated on a particular type of engine and placed all available resources behind its development.

The rejection of Wagner and Müller's work initially angered Hans Mauch since he refused to believe that all their research was worthless and should be discarded without further investigation. Despite this, in July 1939, Junkers received an official development contract for a new axial flow turbojet. The requirement was for it to produce 600 kg (1,320 lbs) thrust at 900 km/h (559 mph) at sea level, or about 700 kg (1,540 lbs) static. Franz was put in charge of this development which possessed no novel or questionable features. It was designed to be brought into production and operation as quickly as possible, and was developed from the outset to burn diesel oil. Franz recalled: "To reduce the risk and ensure success, I decided not to try for the maximum that seemed achievable, but set a rather conservative goal. I believe this approach was one of the main reasons why this completely new type of engine could be developed and put into production in such a short time."

The development of the Junkers engine began in October 1939 under the leadership of Fritz Böttger, with Franz in overall control. To obtain data for the first design, it was decided to build a small-scale engine to allow independent testing of components without excessive expenditure of resources. This was completed in late 1939 but its small scale resulted in inadequate combustion and

△ Anselm Franz (Right) studied mechanical engineering at Graz Technical University. He joined the Junkers engine company in 1936, eventually becoming its chief engineer. After the war he went to America where he worked for the USAF and then for AVCO's Lycoming Division, eventually becoming its vice president.

▽ Photographed at the Luftfahrt Museum at Hannover-Laatzen, this is the only surviving example of a Jumo 004 A-0 pre-production turbojet. Actually the A-022, the engine has its cowlings removed to show its interior details. The object on top is the accessory gearbox used to drive the aircraft's systems.

△ The port Jumo 004 A-0 turbojet (W.Nr.040) of the Ar 234 V2 being test run on the ground. The large cowling door enabled easy maintenance access to the engine.

▽ A view of the eight-stage compressor of the Jumo 004 B-1 engine with the casing removed.

the engine suffered from severe vibration. Independent tests were then made with the compressor alone, but this was wrecked by blade failures during one test at high speed. With the failure of this model, it was decided that studies should be concentrated on a full-size engine, and work on this, the Jumo T 1 (later given the RLM designation 109-004 A) began in December 1939.

In selecting the essential features of the engine it was decided to use an eight-stage compressor, the blade design of which was based on data provided by *Dipl.-Ing.* Encke of the AVA [2] at Göttingen. While Franz was familiar with centrifugal compressors from his supercharger work, he chose an axial-flow system because of its smaller diameter and his conviction that straight-through airflow would be more efficient. Although he felt that an annular combustion chamber would be superior, he selected six individual can-type combustors for the sake of simplicity. For the design of the single-stage turbine wheel, which at first had solid blades, Franz relied on Professor Kraft of AEG [3] in Berlin, this concern having previous experience in the manufacture of steam turbines. From the outset, the exhaust pipe of the turbojet was designed for the later incorporation of after-burning. The engine was equipped with a variable-area exhaust nozzle, mounted in the tailpipe, which could be adjusted to various operating conditions by means of a servo-motor controlled from the throttle lever.

The design of the Jumo T 1 was completed in the spring of 1940, and the prototype made its initial test run on 11 October 1940, without an exhaust nozzle. In December of that year the engine was run at its full design speed of 9,000 rpm, and by the end of January 1941 a thrust of 430 kg (950 lbs) was reached. Considerable problems were then encountered with stator blade

2. *Aerodynamische Versuchsanstalt* (Experimental Institution for Aerodynamics).

3. *Allgemeine Elektrizitäts Gesellschaft* (General Electric Company).

▷ This Jumo 004 B-1 engine was removed from the Ar 234 B-2, W.Nr.140173, of 9./KG 76 which crash landed at Selgersdorf on 23 February 1945. It was later transported to the Royal Aircraft Establishment at Farnborough where it was examined by their specialists and experts from Sir Frank Whittle's Power Jets company.

◁ Another view of the Jumo 004 B-1 taken from the Ar 234 which crash landed at Selgersdorf. This was the first relatively intact German turbojet engine to be captured by the Allies.

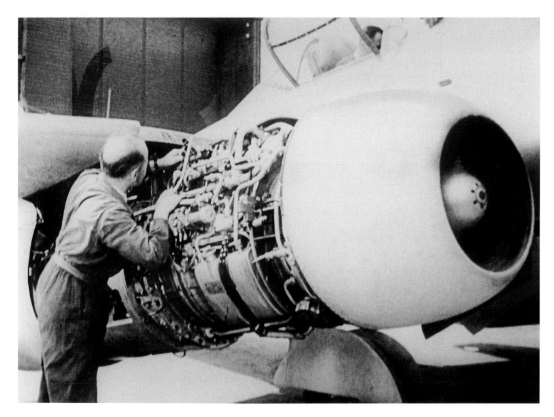

◁ A mechanic makes last minute adjustments to the Jumo 004 V9 engine fitted to the Me 262 V3 prior to that type's first flight on 18 July 1942. As far as is known only four V-series engines were used to power Me 262 prototypes although the prototype engines were flown in at least two test beds.

JUMO 004 V-SERIES PROTOTYPE ENGINES

V1 - V4	Construction began during the autumn of 1939. First test run on 11 October 1940, but suffered many vibration problems. In December 1940 the design rotational speed of 9,000 rpm was attained and also a thrust of 430 kg achieved. On 6 August 1941 the design thrust of 600 kg was achieved and on 24 December 1941 the first ten hour test run was successfully completed. In January 1942 a thrust of 1,000 kg was achieved.
V5	In December 1941 this engine produced a thrust of 1,000 kg (2,200 lbs) for a short period but at unacceptably high temperatures. Later fitted to a Bf 110 test bed and test flown for the first time on 15 March 1942.
V6	
V7	
V8	Me 262 V3 (port) first engine, first flew 18 July 1942, replaced by the A-04 in March 1943 after suffering a turbine failure.
V9	Me 262 V3 (starboard) first engine, first flew 18 July 1942.
V10	
V11	Fitted to a Ju 88 A-4 test bed coded GH+FG.
V12	
V13	Me 262 V2 (probably port - first engine), 1 October 1942, completed 12 hrs 32 min flying, replaced by A-07 in late November 1942 after suffering a turbine failure.
V14	
V15	Me 262 V2 (probably starboard - first engine), 1 October 1942, completed 3 hrs 45 min flying, replaced by A-03.

JUMO 004 A-0 SERIES ENGINES

The first Jumo 004 A-0 engines left the assembly line in late January/early February 1943.

1003 000 001	Probably retained by Junkers for tests.
1003 000 002	Me 262 V3 (starboard – first replacement) first flew with these engines on 20 March 1943. Ten days later the engine failed after 50 meters of the take off run. It was dismantled and examined at Lechfeld and numerous problems found. Replaced on the 31 March 1943 by the A-05.
1003 000 003	Me 262 V2 (starboard – first replacement) completed 8 hrs 47 min flying, replaced by A-05 in late November 1942. Rebuilt and fitted to the Me 262 V3 (port) as the fourth replacement engine. Completed 17 hrs 51 min running.
1003 000 004	Slated for transfer to the *E-Stellen*. Me 262 V3 (port – first replacement) first flew with these engines on 20 March 1943. By 11 April 1943 this engine had completed 11 hrs 21 min flying.
1003 000 005	Me 262 V2 (starboard – second replacement), replaced by the A-010 in February 1943. It would appear that this engine was then fitted to the Me 262 V3 (starboard – second replacement) on 31 March 1943. By 11 April 1943 this engine had completed 8 hrs 31 min flying. Replaced on 7 April by the A-07, already with six hours and 50 minutes at the time of installation.
1003 000 006	Ar 234 V1 – (starboard – first engine), first flew 30 July 1943.
1003 000 007	Me 262 V2 (starboard – second replacement), high temperatures, thrust nozzle replaced, run for 6 hrs 50 min, replaced by the A-010. Later fitted to the Me 262 V3 (starboard – third replacement) on 7 April 1943, run for a total of 17 hrs 51 min by July 1943.
1003 000 008	Development engine for the Jumo 004 B-series.
1003 000 009	Me 262 V2 (port – second replacement), fitted 8 February 1943, completed 13 hrs 39 min by 11 April 1943, replaced by the A-020 in April 1943.
1003 000 010	Me 262 V2 (starboard – third replacement), fitted 8 February 1943, completed 13 hrs 39 min by 11 April 1943, replaced by the A-018 in April 1943. 1003 000 011 He 280 V2 (port), first flew on 16 March 1943.
1003 000 012	He 280 V2 (starboard), first flew on 16 March 1943.
1003 000 013	Development engine for the Jumo 004 B-series, Me 262 V4 (starboard engine) run for 22 hrs by early July 1943.
1003 000 014	
1003 000 015	
1003 000 016 Ar	234 V1 (port – first engine), first flew 30 July 1943, replaced by the A-038.
1003 000 017	Me 262 V4 (port engine) run for 22 hrs 27 min by early July 1943.
1003 000 018	Me 262 V2 (starboard – fourth replacement) this engine introduced an automatic controller for the needle adjustment.

1003 000 019		1003 000 029	
1003 000 020	Me 262 V2 (port – third replacement) this engine introduced an automatic controller for the needle adjustment.	1003 000 030	
		1003 000 031	Ar 234 V4 (port)
1003 000 021		1003 000 032	
1003 000 022		1003 000 033	
1003 000 023	Me 262 V3 (starboard – fourth replacement) run for 10 hrs 51 min.	1003 000 034	
		1003 000 035	Ar 234 V2 (starboard)
1003 000 024		1003 000 036	Ar 234 V4 (starboard)
1003 000 025		1003 000 037	Ar 234 V3 (port)
1003 000 026		1003 000 038	Ar 234 V1 (port – first replacement)
1003 000 027	Originally intended for the Ar 234 V4 (port)	1003 000 039	
1003 000 028	Originally intended for the Ar 234 V4 (port) but fitted to the Ar 234 V3 (starboard)	1003 000 040	Ar 234 V2 (port)

vibration in the compressor which resulted in the prototype engine being almost destroyed through blade failure. Some six months of very laborious work were required before a partial remedy to the vibration problem was found by substituting steel for the original light alloy stator blades. During this period, 15 prototype engines were completed, and on 6 August 1941, the design thrust of 600 kg (1,320 lbs) required was achieved. The first flight of the T 1 in a Bf 110 test bed took place on 15 March 1942. Based on these promising results, the Technical Office issued a contract for 40 T 1 engines, now redesignated Jumo 004 A-0, in the late summer of 1942. These engines, rated at 840 kg (1,850 lbs) thrust, were used for further engine development and airframe application testing in the first prototypes of the Me 262 and the Ar 234.

BMW AND BRAMO

BMW's head of research, *Dr.-Ing.* Kurt Löhner, concentrated on producing a turbojet with a two-stage centrifugal-flow compressor, an annular combustion chamber and a single-stage axial-flow turbine. Difficulties were encountered with this engine, which is believed to have received the project designation P.3301, and it was abandoned at the outbreak of the Second World War.

Bramo's technical director, *Dipl.-Ing.* Bruno Bruckmann and his head of research, *Dr.-Ing.* Hermann Oestrich were initially reluctant to embark on the design of a turbojet, examining the possibilities of using a piston engine to power a ducted fan. Some flight tests were carried out but they proved very disappointing. Consequently it was decided to concentrate all future work on the development of a pure turbojet. This decision was no doubt influenced by the Technical Office placing a development contract, at the beginning of 1939, for a turbojet engine with a static thrust of 600 kg (1,320 lbs) and a diameter of 600 mm (23.6 inches). Shortly afterwards Bramo merged with BMW and all future developments were carried out under the latter's stewardship.

△ Dr. Ing. Hermann Oestrich, with his assistant, Dipl.-Ing. Hermann Hagen, were largely responsible for the development of the BMW P.3302 (later 109-003) turbojet. This was a more advanced engine but suffered a protracted development period before it was used to power the four-engined Ar 234 C and the He 162 Volksjäger.

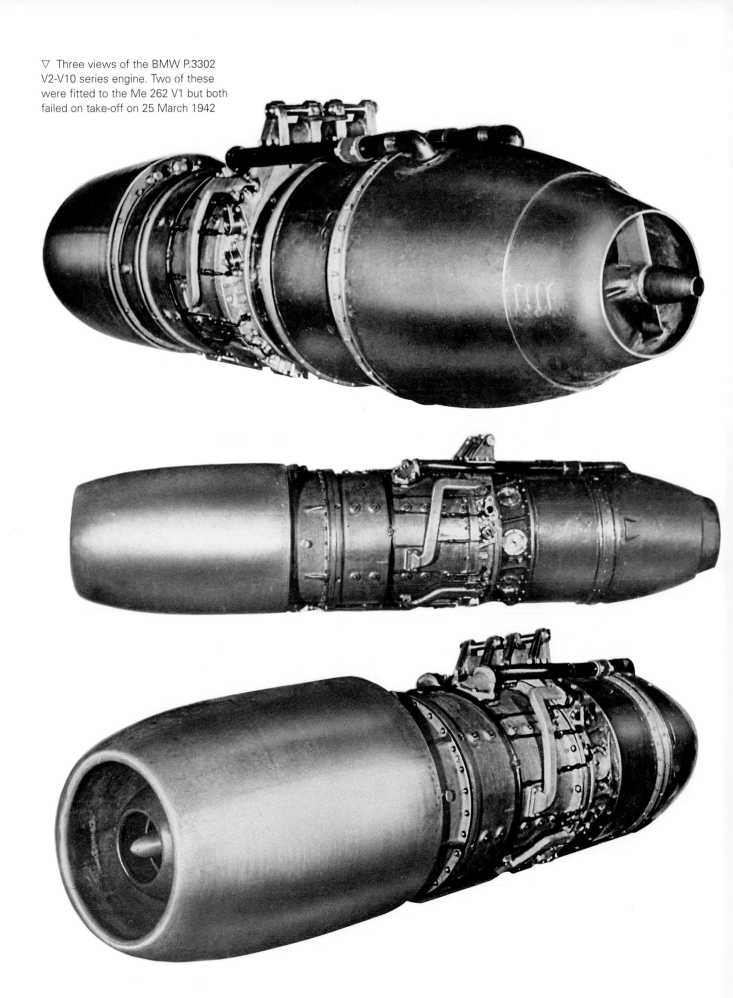

▽ Three views of the BMW P.3302
V2-V10 series engine. Two of these
were fitted to the Me 262 V1 but both
failed on take-off on 25 March 1942

German Class I turbojets

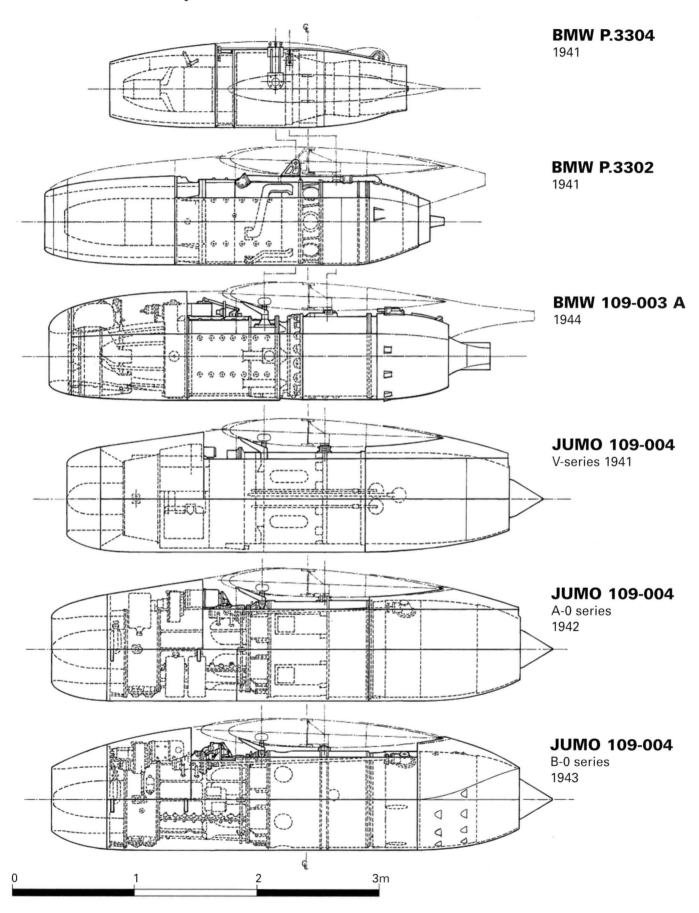

BMW P.3304
1941

BMW P.3302
1941

BMW 109-003 A
1944

JUMO 109-004
V-series 1941

JUMO 109-004
A-0 series
1942

JUMO 109-004
B-0 series
1943

0   1   2   3m

△ The outer casing of this BMW 003 engine has been cutaway to reveal its seven-stage compressor, annular combustion chamber and single-stage turbine. This production engine was considerably improved from the early A-0 engines fitted to the Ar 234 V6 and V8.

Two designs were produced, the complicated P.3304 with a counter-rotating axial-flow compressor and the much more straight-forward P.3302. This was a simple axial-flow engine with a six-stage compressor, annular combustion chamber and a single-stage turbine. Like the competing Jumo T1, it was designed to produce 600 kg (1,320 lbs) thrust at 900 km/h (560 mph) or about 700 kg (1,540 lbs) static thrust at sea level. The P.3304 and P.3302 were given the respective RLM designations 109-002 and 109-003, but the former proved too complex and was finally abandoned in mid-1942.

Many problems were experienced with the BMW 003 as detailed in the table below, but eventually the engine was developed to a point where it could be fitted to the Ar 234.

HEINKEL

Mention should also be made of the work carried out by Hans von Ohain and the Heinkel aircraft company. The young von Ohain patented his turbojet design as early as 9 November 1935 but, lacking the funds necessary for its development, he decided to approach the Heinkel corporation. Ernst Heinkel, an astute businessman, immediately saw the possibilities of the new engine, but withheld details from the RLM's Technical Office.

Early in 1938 detailed design of an aircraft to be powered by von Ohain's engine began under the designation He 178. Two prototypes of this tiny shoulder wing monoplane were to be built, the first with a fixed undercarriage, the second with a retractable unit and an enlarged wing. After considerable development, von Ohain's first practical turbojet, which then developed almost 500 kg (1,100 lbs) thrust was fitted to the He 178 V1. It was this aircraft that carried out the world's first turbojet powered flight on 27 August 1939. Further development of the Heinkel engine led to the HeS 8 (which later received the RLM designation 109-001) that was used to power the world's first jet fighter, the He 280. Despite the success of the Heinkel engines it was the Jumo 004 and BMW 003 that were preferred by the RLM for all operational German jet aircraft.

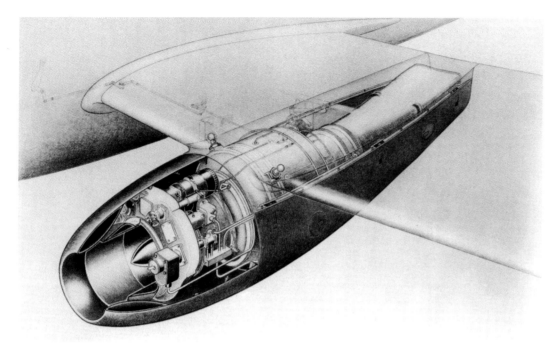

◁ An original airbrushed cutaway drawing showing the installation of the Heinkel-Hirth HeS 8A turbojet mounted beneath the port wing of the He 280 experimental jet fighter. This engine developed 700 kg (1,544 lbs) thrust but it was abandoned in favour of the more promising Junkers and BMW engines.

▽ This cutaway drawing of the HeS 8A (109-001) turbojet gives an excellent impression of the centrifugal flow compressor fitted to this engine. Unlike Britain, Germany quickly abandoned this type of engine in favour of the axial flow design, which is still in use today.

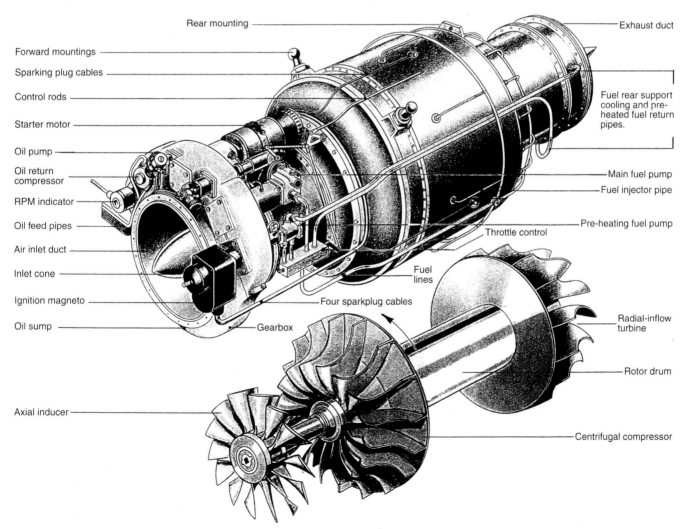

- Rear mounting
- Forward mountings
- Sparking plug cables
- Control rods
- Starter motor
- Oil pump
- Oil return compressor
- RPM indicator
- Oil feed pipes
- Air inlet duct
- Inlet cone
- Ignition magneto
- Oil sump
- Gearbox
- Axial inducer
- Four sparkplug cables
- Fuel lines
- Throttle control
- Exhaust duct
- Fuel rear support cooling and pre-heated fuel return pipes.
- Main fuel pump
- Fuel injector pipe
- Pre-heating fuel pump
- Radial-inflow turbine
- Rotor drum
- Centrifugal compressor

△▽ Taken shortly after completion at Arado's Brandenburg workshops, this photograph shows the twin BMW 003 engine installation on the port side of the Ar 234 V8. These engines were considerably different to those used on the production Ar 234 C-3.

BMW 003 V PROTOTYPE ENGINES

V1   First prototype also known as the P.3302 V1, first ran in December 1940, but the result was very disappointing, only 150 kg (330 lbs) thrust being obtained at 8,000 rpm on the test stand.

V2-V10   During the spring of 1941 a complete redesign of the engine was undertaken, under the generic designation P.3302 V2-V10. A new turbine and combustion chamber was designed and by the summer of 1941 the P.3302 had been persuaded to give 450 kg (990 lbs) thrust on the test stand. Flight trials with a prototype unit began from Berlin-Schönefeld airfield, the turbojet being mounted beneath the fuselage of a Bf 110 twin-engined fighter. Difficulties were still experienced with the turbine wheel, and blade failures occurred at speeds as low as 8,000 rpm due to welding fatigue and heat-induced brittleness. In late November 1941 two P.3302 V2-V10 engines were delivered to Messerschmitt for installation in the Me 262 V1 airframe. By this time improvements had raised static thrust to around 500 kg (1,100 lbs). On 25 March 1942, an unsuccessful test flight took place with the Me 262 V1.

V11-V16   During the spring of 1942, construction commenced on six further experimental engines, designated P.3302 V11-V16, which incorporated the redesign work initiated the previous year. These featured a new seven-stage axial compressor of BMW design with 30 per cent greater airflow. An improved turbine wheel of greatly improved efficiency was also introduced, and overall diameter was increased to 690 mm (26.9 inches). Test stand running of the P.3302 V11 began in the autumn of 1942, and resulted in a thrust of about 550 kg (1,210 lbs). No attempt was made to fly an aircraft under the power of these improved engines, and flights with the P.3302 V11-V16 series were confined to the Bf 110 flying test bed. During the course of these tests a new air intake cowling of improved aerodynamic shape was introduced, and the first trials with a variable-area exhaust nozzle began. Further test stand running with the V11-V16 series eventually increased the thrust to 600 kg (1,320 lbs), as required by the Technical Office development contract, but revealed a number of deficiencies. By the end of 1942, however, solutions had been found, or were within sight, for the most serious difficulties, and a new engine was under development under the designation BMW 003 A-0.

BMW 003 A-0 ENGINES

A-0 no.	W.Nr.	Notes
A-01 – A-09		Experimental engines, no details known.
A-010	010	Fitted to Ju 88 A-5 test bed TH+GE, W.Nr.3255, removed on 8 February 1944.
A-011	011	Replaced W.Nr.010 on Ju 88 TH+GE on 9 February 1944, damaged on 18 February 1944, repair began next day.
A-012 – A-018		Experimental engines, no details known.
A-019	019	Destroyed on 11 December 1943.
A-020		
A-021	386 236	Ar 234 V6 (starboard outer).
A-022	386 237	
A-023	386 238	
A-024	386 239	Ar 234 V8 (starboard outer), later modified to use J 2 fuel, fitted to the Ju 88 in October 1944.
A-025	386 240	Tested on Ju 88 A-5, TH+GE on 14 October 1944.
A-026	386 241	Ar 234 V8 (port outer).
A-027	386 242	
A-028	386 243	Ar 234 V8 (starboard inner), later fitted to Ar 234 V19 (port outer)
A-029	386 244	Ar 234 V8 (port inner).
A-030	386 245	
A-031	386 286	Ar 234 V6 (port inner).
A-032	386 287	Messerschmitt Oberammergau, for Me 262.
A-033	386 288	Ar 234 V6 (starboard inner), apparently later fitted to the Ar 234 V17, starboard, first engine.
A-034	386 289	Ar 234 V6 (port outer).
A-035	386 290	Ar 234 V19 (starboard outer).
A-036	386 291	Messerschmitt Oberammergau, for Me 262.
A-037	386 292	
A-038	386 293	Ar 234 V17 (port) first engine.
A-039	386 294	
A-040	386 295	
A-041	386 751	Tested on Ju 88 A-5, TH+GE on 14 July 1944, still flying September 1944.
A-042	386 752	Under repair on 6 June 1944.

A-043	386 753	Messerschmitt Oberammergau, for Me 262.
A-044	386 754	E-Stelle Rechlin
A-045	386 755	Sagos GmbH, for Ar 234 V17.
A-046	386 753	
A-047	386 754	
A-048	386 755	
A-049	386 759	Sagos GmbH, for Ar 234 V17.
A-050	386 760	Ar 234 V13.
A-051	386 786	E-Stelle Rechlin
A-052	386 787	Messerschmitt Oberammergau, for Me 262.
A-053	386 788	Ar 234 V17 (starboard), November 1944.
A-054	386 789	Betonwerenfabrik, Oranienbaum, for Ju 287 triple engine installation, also given as being fitted to the Ar 234 V19 (starboard inner) second engine.
A-055	386 790	New engine, 5 June 44, fitted with Junkers regulator.
A-056	386 791	Ar 234 V13.
A-057	386 792	New engine, 1 June 1944, fitted with Junkers regulator, repaired on 5 June 44, later fitted to the Ar 234 V13.
A-058	386 793	Fitted to the Ju 88 A-5 TH+GE on 16 June 1944, fitted with Junkers regulator.
A-059	386 794	
A-060	386 795	Betonwerenfabrik, Oranienbaum, for Ju 287 triple engine installation.
A-061	386 796	
A-062	386 797	Replaced A-058 on Ju 88 A-5 TH+GE, September 1944.
A-063	386 798	E-Stelle Rechlin
A-064	386 799	
A-065	386 800	
A-066		
A-067		
A-068		Possibly fitted to the Ju 88 A-5, DG+FR on 1 July 1944.
A-069		
A-070		

A-071	386 851	
A-072	386 852	
A-073	386 853	Junkers, Raguhn for the Ju 287. (given as 386 353).
A-074	386 854	E-Stelle Rechlin
A-075	386 855	Ar 234 V15 (starboard) third engine September/October 1944.
A-076	386 856	Junkers, Raguhn for the Ju 287.
A-077	386 857	
A-078	386 858	Junkers, Raguhn for the Ju 287.
A-079	386 859	Ar 234 V13.
A-080	386 860	
A-081	386 861	
A-082	386 862	
A-083	386 863	
A-084	386 864	
A-085	386 865	
A-086	386 866	Messerschmitt Oberammergau, for Me 262.
A-087	386 867	
A-088	386 868	Ar 234 V14 (starboard) first engine, later to Betonwerenfabrik, Oranienbaum, for Ju 287 triple engine installation.
A-089	386 869	
A-090	386 870	The turbine wheel from this engine is now at the Cranfield Institute of Technology.
A-091	386 896	
A-092	386 897	Ar 234 V15 (port) third engine September/October 1944.
A-093	386 898	Ar 234 V19 (starboard inner) changed after fourth flight to 386789.
A-094	386 899	Junkers, Raguhn for the Ju 287.
A-095	386 900	Ar 234 V14 (port) first engine.
A-096	386 901	
A-097	386 902	
A-098	386 903	
A-099	386 904	
A-0100	386 905	

Design and Development

In the spring of 1940 the RLM's Technical Office asked the Arado company at Brandenburg/Havel to undertake the design of a bomber/photographic reconnaissance aircraft to be powered by the new turbojet engines under development at Junkers and BMW.

In the spring of 1940 no performance details were specified except that the aircraft should be capable of covering Britain as far north as the naval base at Scapa Flow. The specification was largely the result of a suggestion of *Obstlt.* Theodor Rowehl, commander to the *Aufklärunsgruppe Ob.d.L.,* the *Luftwaffe's* clandestine reconnaissance unit.

At this time Arado's Technical Director was Walter Blume, his department comprising the following sections:

TE   *Technische Abteilung – Entwurfsbüro*
(Technical Department – Design office)
under Robert Stelzer.

TEW   *Technische Abteilung – Entwicklung*
(Technical Department – Development)
under *Dipl.-Ing.* Emil Eckstein until the end of 1941 when he was replaced by *Dipl.-Ing.* Wilhelm van Nes with Franz Meyer as his deputy.

TAe   *Technische Abteilung Aerodynamik*
(Technical Department Aerodynamics)
under *Dipl.-Ing.* Rüdiger Kosin.

△ Oberstlt. Theodor Rowehl was one of the Luftwaffe's most important reconnaissance pioneers. He was Kommandeur of the Aufklärungsgruppe Ob.d.L. from its formation on 1 January 1939, and was largely responsible for suggesting the construction of a jet-propelled reconnaissance aircraft which eventually resulted in the Ar 234.

△ Dipl.-Ing. Rüdiger Kosin was born in October 1909 at Neustadt in Westphalia. He joined the Arado company at Brandenburg late in 1936, becoming head of the Aerodynamics Department (TAe) in 1941. He continued to work in the aviation industry after the end of the war, both in Germany and America, eventually becoming Assistant Vice President (Engineering) with the Northrop Company in Los Angeles in December 1968. After returning to Germany he worked for a period with MBB before retiring.

Initial design work on the new project was placed in the hands of Rüdiger Kosin who later recalled: "There was no official requirement for the airplane with the usual accompanying design competition. Only Arado was entrusted with the task of establishing whether an aircraft with the necessary performance was feasible. The number of airplanes planned was fifty. For this reason and his lack of confidence in the new form of propulsion, Walter Blume, Arado's Technical Director, showed little interest in the project. Therefore we, the advanced design department, could work with little interference on a straightforward design."

Design work proceeded under the Arado *Erprobungs* (Experimental) designation E 370. As many as nine alternative proposals were considered, some having four engines and one having a span of 23 metres (75 ft 5 in). A crew of up to four men was also proposed and thought was given to a defensive armament of 13 mm MG 131 machine-guns.

The first definite project, the E 370/IVa, appeared in October 1941. It was a conventional high wing monoplane with a cigar-shaped semi-monocoque fuselage and cruciform tail. Intended for the reconnaissance role, the project was to be

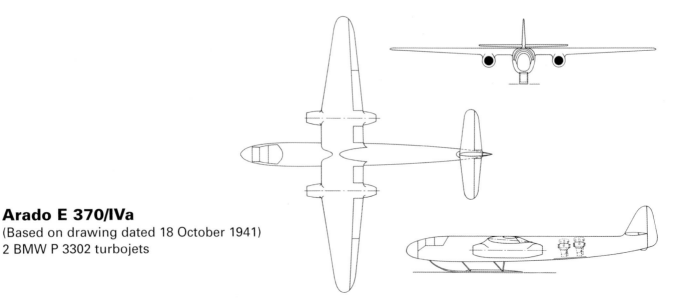

Arado E 370/IVa
(Based on drawing dated 18 October 1941)
2 BMW P 3302 turbojets

▽ An Arado drawing showing the beautifully smooth cast wing panels developed by Rüdiger Kosin's Aerodynamics department for the wing of the E 370/IV project. The idea was to cast the various wing panels in large sections and simply bolt them together. This proposed innovation led the RLM to convene a meeting at Brandenburg to discuss its adoption by other German aircraft manufacturers but in the end the idea was not proceeded with and a more conventional wing construction was adopted.

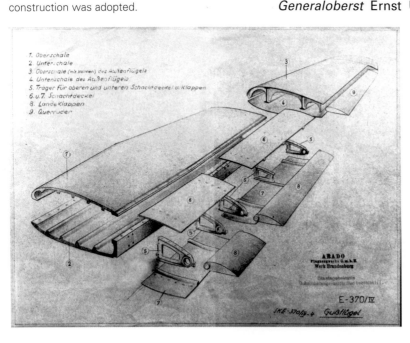

powered by two BMW P 3302 V11 to V14 turbojets slung beneath the wings. Two Rb 50/30 or Rb 75/30 cameras were to be mounted in the rear fuselage and provision was made for a 'token' armament of one 13 mm MG 131 machine-gun. All-up weight was estimated as 7,000 kg (15,432 lbs) which included 4,000 ltrs (880 Imp gals) of fuel in six tanks, three in the fuselage and three in the wing centre section. Because of the need to operate from small military airfields, Kosin's design team proposed that the aircraft take off and land on a broad wooden retractable skid mounted beneath the fuselage.

On 24 October 1941, the design was examined by the RLM's Technical Department and, at a meeting attended by Rowehl, it was decided that an official specification should be issued to cover further development of the project. A batch of 50 aircraft was requested at this stage. The type was envisaged as replacement for the high-altitude Ju 86 R which was then just entering *Luftwaffe* service. A setback came to these plans when *Generaloberst* Ernst Udet, overall head of the Air Ministry's Technical Department, committed suicide on 17 November. His replacement, *Generalfeldmarschall* Erhard Milch, was known to favour continued development of proven types, and this cast doubt upon the future development of the E 370.

By late January 1942 the design had evolved. The fuselage was slightly enlarged and lengthened, with the three fuel tanks contained within the fuselage considerably enlarged in size. The BMW engines, which were experiencing protracted development difficulties, were to be replaced by Jumo 004s with the Daimler-Benz ZTL turbofan (109-007) suggested as a back-up. The skid undercarriage was replaced by a fully-retractable multi-wheeled bogie mounted below the fuselage in an arrangement

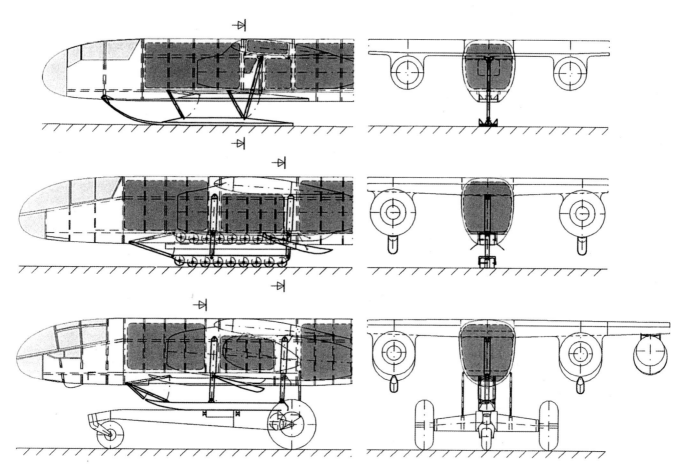

△ Three drawings by Hans-Georg Dachner detailing the development of the undercarriage and fuel tankage for the Arado E 370 /IV project. The top illustration shows the simple retractable fuselage skid without outriggers proposed in October 1941. This project was to be powered by BMW P 3302 turbojets which were of considerably smaller diameter than the later Jumo 004s. The centre drawing illustrates the multi-wheeled semi-retractable bogie arrangement with balancing skids mounted beneath the engines proposed in February 1942. The final drawing shows the jettisonable dolly and retractable skid arrangement of April 1942. This was almost identical to that fitted to the prototype Ar 234 V1. Even at this stage, rocket-assisted take off engines had been added beneath the wings.

▽ A copy of an original Arado Factory drawing showing the side and front views of the E 370/IV project of February 1942 showing the semi-retractable multi-wheeled undercarriage which had previously been fitted to the Ar 232 transport. At this stage the aircraft was to carry two Rb 50/30 cameras in the rear fuselage.

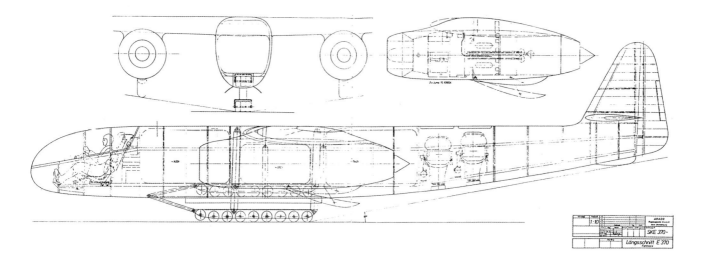

Following the Director General of Equipment, Erhard Milch's, visit to the Arado factory on 4 February 1942, he ordered the construction of a mock-up of the E 370 project, which later became the Ar 234. The views above and left show the completed wooden and *Plexiglas* model of the cockpit area, while that below shows the fuselage still under construction.

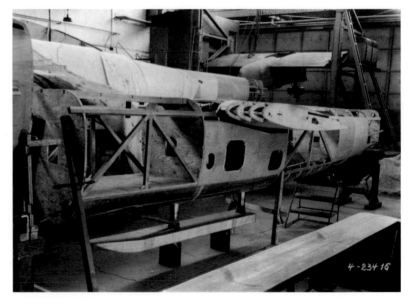

Four views of the mock-up of the rear fuselage of the E 370 showing the Rb 50/30 reconnaissance camera installation. Top left is a view from above of the aft camera, bottom left is another view from above but this time of the forward camera. Top right is a view from below of the rear camera and bottom right is a similar view of the forward camera.

similar to that chosen for the Ar 232 transport. This was balanced by a simple retractable skid mounted below each turbojet. Finally, the wing was completely redesigned. All fuel cells were deleted (leaving the three major fuselage tanks) and constant taper was added to both the leading and trailing edges. More revolutionary was the special wing surface. Rüdiger Kosin explains:

"Up to the design of the E 370 it had been common in the aviation industry to join points of equal percentage in chord, between tip and root, with straight lines. This resulted in warping and unevenness of the sheet metal skinning due to the necessity to rivet it to the spars and ribs. We therefore lofted the wing on the computer [4] by joining points of equal slope, thus obtaining a surface of such smoothness that the RLM ordered all aircraft companies to study our methods at a special meeting held at Brandenburg."

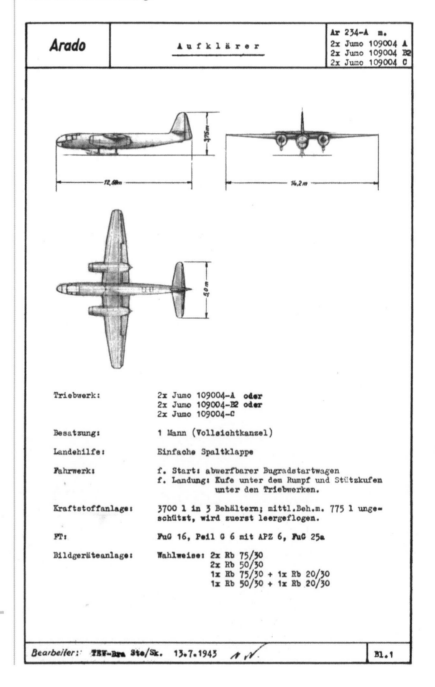

Arado	A u f k l ä r e r	Ar 234-A m. 2x Jumo 109004 A 2x Jumo 109004 B2 2x Jumo 109004 C

Triebwerk: 2x Jumo 109004-A **oder**
                  2x Jumo 109004-B2 **oder**
                  2x Jumo 109004-C

Besatzung: 1 Mann (Vollsichtkanzel)

Landehilfe: Einfache Spaltklappe

Fahrwerk: f. Start: abwerfbarer Bugradstartwagen
                  f. Landung: Kufe unter dem Rumpf und Stützkufen
                              unter den Triebwerken.

Kraftstoffanlage: 3700 l in 3 Behältern; mittl.Beh.m. 775 l unge-
                  schützt, wird zuerst leergeflogen.

FT: FuG 16, Peil G 6 mit APZ 6, FuG 25a

Bildgeräteanlage: Wahlweise: 2x Rb 75/30
                             2x Rb 50/30
                             1x Rb 75/30 + 1x Rb 20/30
                             1x Rb 50/30 + 1x Rb 20/30

Bearbeiter: TEW-Bra Ste/Sk. 13.7.1943   Bl.1

4. At this time, of course, Germany did not possess programmable electronic computers as we know them today, but they did have access to quite sophisticated mechanical calculators.

On 4 February 1942, Erhard Milch visited the Brandenburg Photo Ar234A-089 plant where he was given full details of the revised E 370 by Walter Blume. Milch proved to be extremely impressed by the aircraft and issued a contract covering its structural development and the construction of a wooden mock-up. At the same time the official RLM type '8' series type number '234' was allocated to the project.

▽ Photographed at Arado's Brandenburg/ Neuendorf plant with an Ar 96 in the background the Ar 234 V1 illustrates its sleek lines.

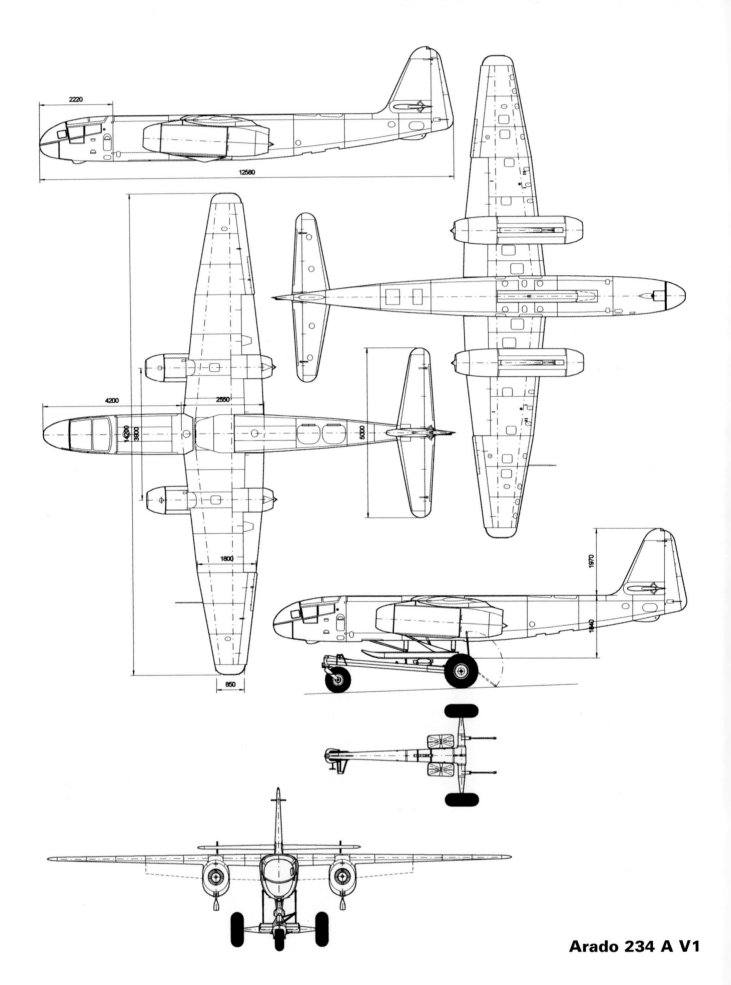

Arado 234 A V1

Two months later the RLM's Technical Department gave preliminary authorisation for the construction of six Ar 234 A prototypes. By this time the project had been further modified. The plan for a retractable skid undercarriage was resurrected but now it was constructed of metal and was to have outriggers beneath each engine. For taxiing and take-off the aircraft was to be provided with a special three-wheeled dolly. This was to be jettisoned after the aircraft left the ground, to fall to earth by parachute where it could be re-used. The dolly weighed 635 kg (1,400 lbs). Provision was also made for jettisonable rocket-assisted take-off units mounted below the wings outboard of the turbojets.

Throughout the remainder of the year a considerable amount of design work and wind tunnel testing of scale models was undertaken in connection with the development of the project. As more details of the turbojets became available, the basic design was updated constantly. Improved fuel consumption figures for the Jumo 004 engine led to a decrease in total fuel tankage to 3,700 ltrs (814 Imp gals). This was housed in three fuselage tanks, those fore and aft being self sealing, that in the centre, unprotected. The only protection for the pilot against enemy fire was a 15 mm armour plate positioned directly behind his head. Dual taper was added to the leading edges of the wing, the area of which was increased, and the control surfaces were revised to incorporate Friese type ailerons of very narrow chord.

The RLM increased its order for Ar 234 prototypes from six to twenty on 28 December 1942. At this stage the V1 to V7 were to be powered by two Jumo 004 engines and to be completed by the end of November 1943. The V8 was to be first test aircraft for four BMW 003 engines and was scheduled to be completed by the end of January 1944. The V9 to V14 (to be built between February and July 1944) were to be powered by two BMW 003s and the V15 to V20 (to be completed between June and October 1944) were to be powered by four BMW 003s.

Construction of the first prototype was begun at the experimental workshops at Brandenburg/Neuendorf on the Havel late in 1942, but because of difficulties with the development of the Jumo 004 turbojets it was not until February 1943 that the first pair of these arrived. Although nominally producing 850 kg (1,874 lbs) thrust the early engines rarely managed to achieve this power. Thought was therefore given to various methods of boosting available take-off power. One scheme, evolved in conjunction with the Graf Zeppelin Research Institute at Stuttgart-Ruit, envisaged using He 111 H-6 bombers as tugs. This scheme was abandoned in favour of that proposed earlier using two Walter 109-500 rocket-assisted take-off engines mounted beneath each wing. These were capable of delivering a thrust of 500 kg (1,102 lbs) thrust for thirty seconds.

During the early summer of 1943, some static engine testing and taxiing trials were carried out with the first prototype, the Ar 234 V1. It was known that the runway at Brandenburg was too short for flight trials with such an advanced aircraft, and a new, specially-constructed strip at Alt Lönnewitz was not ready. Alt Lönnewitz was a former *Luftwaffe* base in Saxony, about 65 km (40 miles) north-west of Dresden.

△ For taxiing trials carried out towards the end of July 1943 at Rheine airfield a small cycle wheel was mounted behind the take-off dolly for measurement purposes.

Therefore the prototype was dismantled and ferried to a *Luftwaffe* airfield at Rheine near Münster in an Ar 232 transport. Arriving there on 18 July, it was reassembled to undergo a further series of taxiing trials during the next seven days. These were mainly concerned with the stability of the take-off dolly.

On 26 July the port engine caught fire at over 3000 rpm owing to a leak in the injectors. The engine had to be removed, but was quickly repaired by Junkers engineers and refitted two days later. During the evening of 30 July the aircraft made its first successful test flight with the experienced Arado test pilot, *Flugkapitän* Horst Selle, at the controls. With the take-off weight limited to 5,695 kg (12,555 lbs) no rocket assistance was required. Selle released the dolly successfully at about 600 metres (2,000 ft) but after deployment the parachute became entangled in the supporting struts at the rear and the dolly was destroyed when it hit the ground. Otherwise the 14 minute flight went without a hitch.

During static testing on 7 August the troublesome port engine was found to be leaking again. A replacement (removed from the almost complete V3) was flown in from Brandenburg and fitted the following day. Two days later, Selle flew the prototype for the second time, attaining a speed of 650 km/h (404 mph) during a test lasting 54 minutes. In an attempt to prevent the loss of a second take-off dolly the parachute container was moved further forward, but again it failed to deploy. The dolly was modified a third time by mounting the parachute container *behind* the main wheels and it was also decided to release it immediately following take-off. This procedure was first tested during the third flight of the V1 and, having proved successful, was adopted for all subsequent flights.

Following the completion of this third flight, on 29 August 1943, Selle mishandled the throttles on landing, causing the aircraft to overshoot the grass strip by some 160 metres (525 ft). The prototype was so badly damaged during the subsequent belly landing that it never flew again. Some parts from the wreckage were salvaged including the rear fuselage which was placed at the disposal of Frieseke und Höpfner for the trial installation of a new type of ceramic radio aerial.

Shortly afterwards the Ar 234 V2 was completed. This was virtually identical to the first prototype with a similar type of dolly to that used on that aircraft's last flight. During static tests on 7 September, both engines of the V2 were found to be faulty and had to be replaced. Six days later, Selle ferried the airplane from Brandenburg to Alt Lönnewitz to where the Ar 234 flight test program had now been transferred. Three further flights totalling 1 hour 41 minutes followed on the 14th, 16th and 23rd, these being mainly concerned with engine measurements.

Work was now progressing on the Ar 234 V3 which was designed to be fitted with a pressurized cabin and an ejector

seat although these were never installed. The prototype also had a redesigned take-off dolly with large outriggers mounted on each side which supported the auxiliary skids beneath the turbojets. It was flown for the first time on 29 September 1943 with Selle ferrying the prototype from Brandenburg to Alt Lönnewitz in only 21 minutes. A second, 51 minute, flight in the aircraft the following day resulted in damage to the take-off dolly after it was released at an altitude in excess of 2 metres (6 ft 6 ins).

On 1 October 1943, Selle made his fifth flight in the Ar 234 V2, but it was to prove his last. At first there was some doubt as to the cause of the crash, but this was finally resolved at an Office of Air Armaments conference held five days later. Selle's brief had been to make an ascent to 9,000 metres (29,500 ft) to check the aircraft's climbing capability. He remained in radio contact with the ground until the last moment. Although he bravely tried to save the prototype, his efforts were in vain. At the last moment he jettisoned the escape hatch in an attempt to bale out but, by then, it was too late.

Following the fire and subsequent crash of the V2, a report was issued on 19 October 1943 which called for the installation of automatic fire extinguishing equipment in the V3 and ejector seats in the V3, V4, V5, V8, V9, V10, V11, V15, V16 and V17. This compressed air-activated seat had been designed by the Heinkel company for its He 280 fighter, but was to be modified for the Ar 234. Despite the call for such a device, no Ar 234 was actually fitted with it but operational experience was to show that bailing out from the aircraft through the small entry hatch in the top of the canopy was far from easy.

Flight testing of the Ar 234 V3 did not resume until 11 November 1943 when Arado's chief test pilot, *Flugkapitän* Walter Kröger, made his first flight in the prototype. On the next day *Flugkapitän* Johann Ubbo Janssen, who had joined Arado on 13 September 1943, flew the V3 from Alt Lönnewitz to Jüterbog, but problems with the port engine encountered during the flight prevented its return until 15 November.

◁△ The Ar 234 V2, W.Nr.130002, was virtually identical to the V1 and could only be distinguished externally by its four letter code DP+AW.
The Ar 234 A-series prototypes were virtually hand-built and possessed a beautifully smooth external finish.

▽ Although the Ar 234 V3 airframe was very similar to the previous two prototypes, its take-off dolly was considerably different. It had large outriggers supporting the auxiliary skids beneath the turbojets which much improved stability while taxiing on the concrete runway.

△ The Ar 234 V4, W.Nr.130004, coded DP+AY, was very similar to the third prototype. It is shown here just after completion with the Walter 109-500 rocket-assisted take-off pods in place.

Six days later the V3 was dismantled and transferred by road to Insterburg in East Prussia where it was to take part in a demonstration in front of Adolf Hitler of the latest types of German aircraft and equipment. Apart from the Ar 234 V3 the display included the Me 262 V1 and V6, the Me 163 BV22 rocket fighter, an example of the V-1 flying bomb and several experimental guided missiles. Hitler arrived in his special train at 11 am and following a tour of the exhibition, both the Me 262 V6 and Me 163 were demonstrated, the former by Gerd Lindner, the latter by Bernhard Hohmann. The Ar 234 was not flown, but the Führer was so impressed with the design that he ordered the production of at least 200 aircraft by the end of 1944.

The fourth prototype, the Ar 234 V4, was generally similar to the previous aircraft. It was completed on 24 October 1943, but flight testing was delayed because of the need to carry out

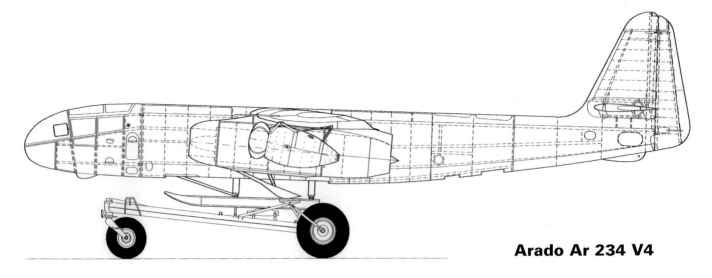

Arado Ar 234 V4

extensive engine evaluation. The aircraft finally made its first flight on 26 November, taking off with the aid of rocket-assistance. Even then Janssen experienced problems with the port engine during taxiing.

Following its return from Insterburg, the V3 had been fitted with a special toothed landing skid with the idea of slowing the aircraft's landing run. It was first tested on 18 December when it landed on the snow covered airfield at Alt Lönnewitz and proved quite successful. On 24 February 1944, the V3 made the first of several tests of a braking parachute which, when deployed, considerably reduced the landing run.

Meanwhile the Ar 234 V5 had been completed. This differed from the earlier prototypes in having modified landing skids and Jumo 004 B-0 engines. Although producing a similar thrust to the A-series engines, these were some 100 kg (220 lbs) lighter. Janssen carried out the first flight of the V5 on 22 December 1943 with the aid of rocket assistance. However, as he brought the aircraft in to land at Alt Lönnewitz, he discovered that he could not reduce the engines to idling speed and was forced to make a very fast approach, skimming across the concrete runway. This caused the skids to collapse which in turn damaged the wingtips and port wing. Nevertheless the pilot had a good impression of the V5's flight characteristics. After being repaired, the prototype was flown for a second time on 20 January 1944, but as a safety precaution, the skids were locked down.

During January and February 1944, Janssen carried out several flights in the Ar 234 V3, V4 and V5. One of these was on 20 January when he ferried the V4 to Brandenburg-Havel to await the arrival of Erhard Milch and Karl-Otto Saur. Milch (Director General of *Luftwaffe* Equipment) and Saur (deputy to Speer – Hitler's Armament Minister) were touring Germany by special train to check on production arrangements for the Ar 234, Me 262 and Do 335. The two officials and their entourage visited the Arado factory on 21 January where Janssen treated them to a 25 minute demonstration flight in the Ar 234 V4 before returning it to Alt Lönnewitz.

▽ The Ar 234 V5, W.Nr.130005, was the first prototype to be fitted with the much lighter Jumo 004 B-0 pre-production turbojets. It also differed in having more substantial landing skids.

Following the completion of four flights in the Ar 234 V5 by Janssen, the aircraft was flown by *Obstlt.* Siegfried Knemeyer on 9 February. Knemeyer had been appointed *Entwicklungs-Chef* (Head of Development) in the RLM's *Technisches Amt* (Technical Department) usually abbreviated to *Chef GL/C-E* in November 1943. This was one of the most important positions in the *Generalluftzeugmeister's* organisation with responsibility for the development of all new and existing *Luftwaffe* equipment. As part of this job, he became responsible for the direction of all jet aircraft development until the end of the war.

During another flight, on 22 February, Janssen tested modified snow skids on the Ar 234 V5, but they caught in ruts on landing and collapsed, shattering the cockpit glazing. This failure led to their abandonment. At this stage many problems were being experienced with the skids collapsing and, in an attempt to solve the problem, Hans Rebeski, departmental head of detailed design, suggested that they be raised and lowered twice before landing to ensure hydraulic pressure was at its maximum. This procedure was first tried on the V3 and seemed to overcome the problem.

After being repaired, the V5 rejoined the test program only to be damaged again on 2 April following its eighth flight. Janssen took off successfully from Alt Lönnewitz, but found he could not release the dolly and was forced to land at Brandenburg with it still attached. Without the dolly brakes connected the prototype hurtled off the runway, eventually shuddering to a halt in a field. As if in slow motion, it slid from its dolly, damaging the underside of the fuselage.

Because of the increasing tempo of Ar 234 prototype testing a second test pilot was appointed to assist Ubbo Janssen. Günther Eheim. He had joined the company in March 1944 from the bomber *Geschwader* KG 40 and made his first flight in the Ar 234, the V5, on 24 April.

It will be remembered that the BMW P.3302 (109-003) had been proposed for the Arado E 370 project from its inception. Early problems with this engine, which was more advanced in concept than the Jumo 004, had delayed its introduction. During the summer of 1943, however, Kosin's team began to consider a version of the Ar 234 to be powered by four BMW engines. As Kosin explained:

▽   The Ar 234 V8, W.Nr. 130008, coded GK+IY, which was powered by four 109-003 A-0 engines in combined nacelles. These early BMW engines were extremely unreliable and posed constant problems.

"In order to accommodate four of the smaller, lighter and less powerful engines, two solutions were considered. The first was to pair the engines in the same position as the Jumo 004s, the second to mount a single turbojet at this point and another outboard at the existing hard points for the rocket-assisted take-off units. Any modification to the wing was absolutely out of the question. Structurally, the single engine solution was preferable, but from the point of view of stability, control and handling qualities, it appeared less desirable. Flight testing was to confirm our calculations."

Preliminary performance figures for the project looked promising, including a maximum speed of 860 km/h (534 mph) at 4,000 m (13,000 ft) and a range of 1470 km (913 miles) at 12,000 m (39,370 ft). In order to determine the most efficient arrangement of the two layouts proposed by Kosin, two Ar 234 A-series prototypes were allocated.

The first of these to be completed was the Ar 234 V8 which was intended to test the combined nacelle arrangement. The centreline of the new combined twin engine installation used the original mounting points for the single Jumo engines. This meant that the dolly outriggers which supported the skids under the outboard engines had to be slightly extended. Otherwise the take-off and landing arrangement was similar to the earlier prototypes.

Janssen flew the Ar 234 V8 for the first time on 4 February 1944, thus gaining the distinction of making the world's first four-jet flight. Subsequent flight testing was hampered by the unreliability of the BMW engines. An earlier version of the engine had previously been tested in the Me 262 V1 but this had failed on take-off and was extensively redesigned. The new BMW 003 A-0 engines were tested on a Ju 88 test bed, but even then major problems were experienced, mainly due to the unsatisfactory regulator governors and the Henschel-designed fuel pumps. By 17 April 1944 the V8 had completed only 79 minutes flying.

A second four-engined prototype, the Ar 234 V6, was completed a little later. This was fitted with four BMW 003 engines in separate nacelles and was flight cleared on 17 April 1944. It made its first flight eight days later but its engines proved just as troublesome as those fitted to the V8. On 11 May, Arado expressed grave doubts about the safety of both aircraft and were already considering abandoning flight testing when all four turbojets of the V6 suffered successive failures on 1 June. This event forced Ubbo Janssen to crash land the aircraft onto the Torgau-Eilenberg railway line which resulted in minor damage. No further flights were made with the two four-engined prototypes although comparison flights had shown, as Kosin

△▽ The V6, W.Nr.130006, coded GK+IW, was the only Ar 234 to be powered by four BMW 003 A-0 engines in four separate cowlings. It was intended that this prototype would conduct comparison tests with the V8 to determine the best power plant arrangement. Although only seven flights were conducted with the V6 and six with the V8, they did prove that the combined nacelle arrangement was much better. Subsequently this arrangement was tested on a B-series airframe, the Ar 234 V13, and later it was adopted by Ar 234 C-3 production model.

Arado Ar 234 V6

This aircraft was powered by four BMW 003 A-0 engines in separate nacelles. Retractable balancing skids were mounted beneath each of the four engines

had predicted, that the combined nacelle arrangement was superior. They also paved the way for the Ar 234 C-series.

On 23 May 1944 *Hptm.* Conny Noell of the *Versuchsverband OKL* suggested the making available of two Ar 234 prototypes to undertake experimental reconnaissance operations over the invasion beaches. As Noell said: "It was the ideal reconnaissance aircraft." Three days later, during discussions between *Dipl.-Ing.* Liebing of Arado, *Obstlt.* Knemeyer of the RLM and *Oberst* Petersen of the *Luftwaffe's Erprobungstellen* (Experimental Stations), the plan was accepted.

Arado technicians at Brandenburg immediately began work to mount a pair of Rb 50/30 cameras in the rear fuselage of the Ar 234 V5 (GK+IV). Following completion of this test pilot Ubbo Janssen flew the machine to Alt Lönnewitz on 1 June 1944. The second prototype to be fitted with cameras was the only other Jumo-powered A-series airframe to be completed, the Ar 234 V7. Basically similar to the V5 it was fitted from the outset with two Rb 50/30 cameras in the rear fuselage. It made its first flight on 22 June 1944 with chief test pilot Walter Kröger at the controls, but the rear support strut for the main skid collapsed on landing due to a hydraulic fault.

Arado Ar 234 V5

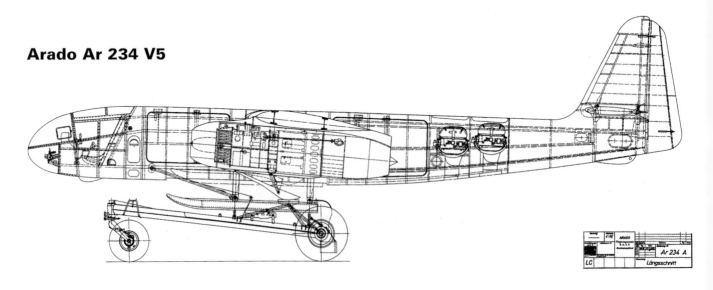

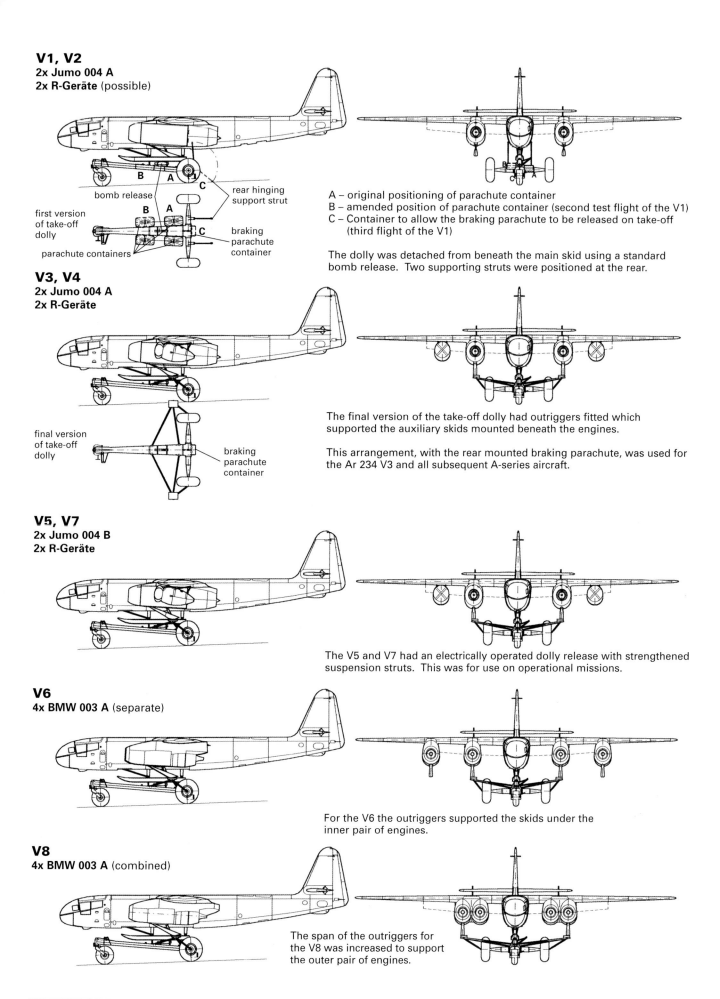

V1, V2
2x Jumo 004 A
2x R-Geräte (possible)

bomb release

rear hinging
support strut

first version
of take-off
dolly

braking
parachute
container

parachute containers

A – original positioning of parachute container
B – amended position of parachute container (second test flight of the V1)
C – Container to allow the braking parachute to be released on take-off
(third flight of the V1)

The dolly was detached from beneath the main skid using a standard
bomb release. Two supporting struts were positioned at the rear.

V3, V4
2x Jumo 004 A
2x R-Geräte

final version
of take-off
dolly

braking
parachute
container

The final version of the take-off dolly had outriggers fitted which
supported the auxiliary skids mounted beneath the engines.

This arrangement, with the rear mounted braking parachute, was used for
the Ar 234 V3 and all subsequent A-series aircraft.

V5, V7
2x Jumo 004 B
2x R-Geräte

The V5 and V7 had an electrically operated dolly release with strengthened
suspension struts. This was for use on operational missions.

V6
4x BMW 003 A (separate)

For the V6 the outriggers supported the skids under the
inner pair of engines.

V8
4x BMW 003 A (combined)

The span of the outriggers for
the V8 was increased to support
the outer pair of engines.

△ These views of the Ar 234 V1 show the lack of outriggers to support the turbojet skids which were introduced later on the third prototype. Also clearly visible in these views are the two hinged struts at the back of the dolly which supported the rear fuselage.

◁ The Ar 234 V1, TG+KB, passes alongside a flak emplacement at Rheine airfield in the summer of 1943 during taxiing trials.

▷ On its second flight on 30 July 1943, piloted by test pilot Horst Selle, the brake parachute of the Ar 234 V1 take-off dolly became entangled in the support struts at the rear, causing it to be destroyed.

◁ A dramatic photograph showing the Ar 234 V1 taking off on its third flight. For the first time, the dolly was released just after take-off at about 150 km/h (90 mph) and landed successfully. As can be seen from the unpainted nose of the port turbojet cowling, this engine had been changed on 7 August 1943.

△ Front view of the Ar 234 V3 showing the modified take-off dolly with outriggers to support the balancing skids beneath the turbojets.

▽ The port Jumo 004 A-0 turbojet (W.Nr. 040) of the Ar 234 V2 being test run on the ground. The large cowling door enabled easy maintenance access to the engine.

△△▷ A sequence of photographs showing the Ar 234 V2 with its skids extended landing on the grass strip at Alt Lönnewitz during the late summer of 1943. After touching down, the aircraft would tip from side to side on its balancing skids before finally slewing to a halt.

△▷▽ Three views of the Ar 234 V3 taking off from Alt Lönnewitz airfield. As the prototype leaves the concrete runway, the dolly is jettisoned to be slowed by its braking parachute.

△▷▽ A sequence of stills extracted from an Arado cine film showing the Ar 234 V3 landing on the grass strip at Alt Lönnewitz in Lower Saxony. After slewing to a halt on its skids, two trucks hurry out to retrieve the aircraft while the pilot climbs from the glazed hatch in the top of the canopy. The truck on the left is towing the take-off dolly, on to which the aircraft had to be returned before it could be towed back to its dispersal. The vehicle on the right is a refuelling tanker.

◁ This photograph of the Ar 234 V4 should be compared with that at the top of page 40. It clearly shows the differences between the take off dollys of the first two prototypes and the V3 and V4.

▽ Both Horst Götz and Erich Sommer made several familiarisation flights in the Ar 234 V4, coded DP+AY, before they were ready for action in France. The fourth prototype differed from the two operational A-series aircraft, the V5 and V7, by being powered by Jumo 004 A-0 engines and also had slightly modified skids under the engines.

▷▽ The V4 made its first flight on 26 November 1943 piloted by Flugkapitän Ubbo Janssen. The prototype is shown just before touching down at Alt Lönnewitz after an early flight. Because of the skid undercarriage the aircraft had to land on a grass strip.

◁▽ During an early flight in the Ar 234 V5 on 2 April 1944, *Flugkapitän* Ubbo Janssen found that he could not release the take-off dolly and he was forced to land with it still attached. The photograph above shows the aircraft taking off on this flight, that below it landing with the fuselage main skid under compression. Unfortunately the dolly skids had been disconnected and the V5 careered along the runway out of control eventually coming to a halt in some woods.

▷ The Ar 234 V7, now coded T9+MH, in the operational markings of *Kommando Götz*, lands at Rheine airfield not long before the aircraft was retired from service. The V7 and V5 were essentially similar.

▷ With its take-off dolly in the foreground, the Ar 234 V7 is prepared for an operational sortie. The cockpit glazing has been protected by a purpose made covering sheet.

△▽▷ The V6, W.Nr. 130006, coded GK+IW, was the only Ar 234 to be powered by four BMW 003 A-0 engines in four separate cowlings. It was intended that this prototype would conduct comparison tests with the V8 to determine the best power plant arrangement. Although only seven flights were conducted with the V6 and six with the V8, they did prove that the combined nacelle arrangement was much better. Subsequently this arrangement was tested on a B-series airframe, the Ar 234 V13, and later it was adopted by Ar 234 C-3 production model.

The Ar 234 V8, W.Nr. 130008, coded GK+IY, was the world's first four-jet aircraft, powered by four 109-003 A-0 engines in combined nacelles. These early BMW engines were extremely unreliable and posed constant problems.

◁△△◁ A sequence of photographs showing the take off of the Ar 234 V8 from Alt Lönnewitz during the spring of 1944. After leaving the ground, the dolly is jettisoned and its braking parachute deployed. In the lower photograph the aircraft climbs away, still with its main skid extended. Apart from its engines the aircraft was very similar to the V5.

Airframe and Equipment

The Ar 234 was a conventional shoulder-wing monoplane of clean aerodynamic design.

The fuselage of the Arado Ar 234 was a semi-monocoque structure with flat 'top hat' section longerons and 'Z' section formers and stringers. The fully-glazed cockpit area was provided with a small entrance hatch in the roof which hinged to starboard. Although adequate for normal entry, its small dimensions were to prove a problem during operations when the pilot was forced to bail out. His only protection from enemy gunfire was a 15 mm thick armour plate mounted behind his head. The forward self-sealing fuel tank was mounted directly behind the cockpit, containing 1,800 litres (396 Imp. gallons). Three oxygen bottles were sandwiched between this tank and the forward bulkhead. The rear fuel tank was positioned behind the wing and housed 2,000 litres (440 Imp. gallons) of J2. Both fuel tanks had their filler points in the fuselage top decking.

Two Rb 50/30 cameras were mounted one behind the other in the rear fuselage behind the after fuel tank. They were fitted with a 50 cm telephoto lens, and took a 30 cm (11.8 inch) square picture. They both pointed downwards and were splayed at 12 degrees to the vertical. Thus, from an altitude of 10,000 m (33,000 ft), the cameras were able to cover a swathe of ground

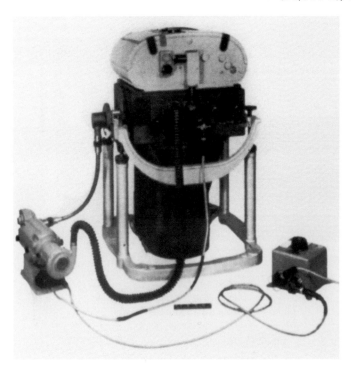

△ The Rb 50/30 automatic reconnaissance camera, seen here mounted in its servicing cradle, weighed 72.5 kg (160 lbs). The pale coloured object at the top of the camera is the removable film magazine which, when fully loaded, could contain 65 m (213 ft) of film.

▷ Taken from above, this photograph shows the two Rb 50/30s mounted in the rear fuselage camera bay of the Ar 234. These were mounted 12 degrees from the vertical, enabling the aircraft, when flying at 10,000 m (33,000 ft), to cover a strip of ground 10 km (6 miles) wide.

just over 10 km (6 miles) wide along the aircraft's track. The film magazines were mounted above each camera for easy removal via a hatch in the top of the fuselage.

The wing had two main spars and 29 ribs, the all-metal structure covered in stressed-skin. It could be detached from the fuselage by the removal of four large bolts. Two sets of hydraulically-operated flaps were mounted in the rear of the wing, on either side of the turbojets. The Friese-type ailerons were of exceptionally narrow chord and positioned immediately outboard of the flaps. They were fitted with small mass-balanced geared tabs. Hard points were provided outboard of the engines beneath which could be slung a Walter 109-500 rocket-assisted take-off unit. These were capable of delivering a thrust of 500 kg (1,102 lbs) thrust for thirty seconds. After use they were jettisoned to fall to earth with the aid of a parachute mounted on the nose.

The cruciform tail was also built of metal with stressed-skin covering. The full length rudder was fitted with a Flettner tab above and a normal geared tab below. The elevators were also of full width with three-quarter length geared tabs.

Two Jumo 004 A-0 engines were mounted below the wings of the Ar 234 V1 to V4, these delivering 840 kg (1,850 lbs) thrust at 9,000 rpm. The V5 and V7 were powered by the improved and lighter Jumo 004 B-0 engines which delivered 900 kg (1,980 lbs) thrust. Both engines were 3.80 m (12 ft 5¹/₂ ins) long, had a diameter of 0.96 m (3 ft 1¹/₂ ins) and were attached to the wing spars by three mounting bolts. The A-0 weighed 850 kg (1,874 lbs), the B-0 being some 100 kg (220 lbs) lighter. Each had an eight-stage axial-flow compressor, six separate combustion chambers and a single-stage turbine. A feature of the turbojet was the movable cone at the rear to control thrust. The engines were started using a Riedel AK 11 two-stroke motor mounted in the forward central 'bullet' housing. This engine was in turn started using a lawnmower-like pull handle.

Unlike the other A-series prototypes, the Ar 234 V6 and V8 were powered by four BMW 003 A-0 turbojets. This engine had a seven-stage axial-flow compressor, an annular combustion chamber and a single-stage turbine. The engine developed a thrust of 800 kg (1,764 lbs) at 9,500 rpm and weighed 570 kg (1,257 lbs). It was 3.565 m (11 ft 8¹/₂ ins) long (with the exhaust bullet extended) and had a diameter of 0.69 m (2 ft 3 ins). Unlike the Jumo 004, the early BMW engines used B4 petrol rather than J2 heavy oil fuel.

The jettisonable take-off dolly weighed 640 kg (1,411 lbs) and was of tricycle layout. It had a self-centring nosewheel and was steered by use of brakes and the aircraft's engines. Hydraulic brakes were provided on the main wheels, operated via the rudder panels. On take-off, the dolly was released by a red handle in the cockpit, the hydraulic couplings to the brakes disconnecting and automatically sealing themselves. After being jettisoned, the dolly was slowed by a braking parachute

▽ The Riedel AK 11 two-cylinder, two-stroke petrol engine which was used to start the smaller German turbojet engines such as the Jumo 004. The engine was itself started by the use of a small pull ring handle similar to that fitted to a lawnmower.

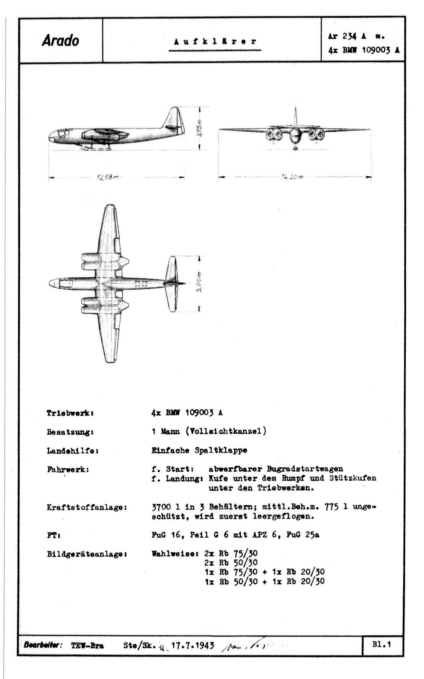

▷ An Arado drawing taken from a document dated 17 July 1943 showing the basic layout of the proposed Ar 234 A model powered by four BMW 003 A engines in combined nacelles. As can be seen, various camera combinations were proposed.

| Arado | A u f k l ä r e r | Ar 234 A m. |
| | | 4x BMW 109003 A |

Triebwerk:	4x BMW 109003 A
Besatzung:	1 Mann (Vollsichtkanzel)
Landehilfe:	Einfache Spaltklappe
Fahrwerk:	f. Start: abwerfbarer Bugradstartwagen
	f. Landung: Kufe unter dem Rumpf und Stützkufen unter den Triebwerken.
Kraftstoffanlage:	3700 l in 3 Behältern; mittl.Beh.m. 775 l ungeschützt, wird zuerst leergeflogen.
FT:	FuG 16, Peil G 6 mit APZ 6, FuG 25a
Bildgeräteanlage:	Wahlweise: 2x Rb 75/30
	2x Rb 50/30
	1x Rb 75/30 + 1x Rb 20/30
	1x Rb 50/30 + 1x Rb 20/30

| Bearbeiter: TEW-Bra   Ste/Sk. 4 17.7.1943 | B1.1 |

stowed in a box at the rear. The system was developed with the help of the Parachute Training School at Wittstock. Due to the difficulties with the quick release mechanism, it was decided on the first flights not to jettison the dolly until the airplane had attained an altitude of several hundred feet. It would then be released to fall to the ground with the aid of a parachute. However, this proved unsatisfactory and on all subsequent tests and operations it was released just after take-off, a parachute being deployed to ensure that it did not hit the aircraft.

Radio equipment for the Ar 234 A comprised an FuG 16 ZY transceiver. This used a simple wire aerial positioned between the centre of the fuselage upper decking and the top of the fin with an additional feed to the radio itself which was mounted in the rear fuselage. The later B-series introduced the FuG 25 direction-finding device with its aerial mounted above the wing centre section.

Arado Ar 234 V4 Specification

	metric	Imperial
Engines		

Two Junkers 004 A-0 turbojets rated at 840 kg (1,852 kg) static thrust at 9,000 rpm.

	metric	Imperial
Length	3.80 m	12 ft 5$\frac{1}{2}$ ins
Diameter	0.96 m	3 ft 1$\frac{3}{4}$ ins
Weight	850 kg	1,874 lbs

Two Walter 109-500 rocket-assisted take-off engines mounted beneath each wing producing 500 kg (1,102 lbs) thrust for thirty seconds.

Airframe Dimensions

	metric	Imperial
Wing span	14.20 m	46 ft 7 ins
Wing area	26.40 m^2	284.18 sq ft
Tailplane span	5.00 m	16 ft 3$\frac{3}{4}$ ins
Fuselage length	12.56 m	41 ft 2$\frac{1}{2}$ ins
Height (top of fin to extended skid)	3.81 m	12 ft 6 ins

Weights

	metric	Imperial
Airframe	2,150 kg	4,740 lbs
Engines (including cowlings, starters etc)	2,100 kg	4,630 lbs
Total	*4,250 kg*	*9,370 lbs*
Equipment	500 kg	1,102 lbs
Basic weight	4,750 kg	10,472 lbs
Pilot	100 kg	220 lbs

Fuel

	metric	Imperial
Forward fuel tank	1,800 litres	(396 Imp gals)
Rear fuel tank	2,000 litres	(440 Imp gals)
Total fuel weight	*3,800 kg*	*8,377 lbs*
Riedel starter fuel	20 kg	44 lbs
Oil	30 kg	66 lbs
Flying weight	8,700 kg	19,179 lbs
Flying weight with take-off dolly	9,340 kg	20,590 lbs
Flying weight with dolly and RATO	9,900 kg	21,825 lbs

Performance

	metric	Imperial
Maximum speed	760 km/h	472 mph
Maximum range (approx)	1,500 km	932 miles

Armament and cameras

	metric	Imperial
	none	none

The dolly arrangement
designed for the Ar 234 V5 and V7

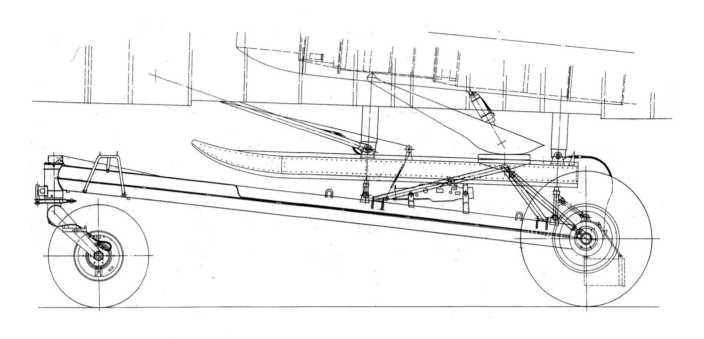

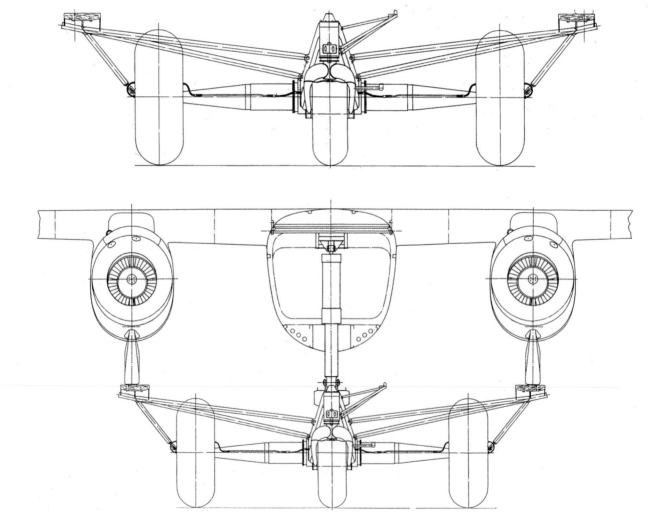

◁ An excellent close-up view of the take-off dolly fitted to the Ar 234 V5. This was very similar to that used by the V3 and V4 but had strengthened support struts.

▷ The front of the dolly was fitted with a castering nosewheel. The struts protruding from the mainwheel support and from the forward part of the main body of the skid were steps to enable pilots and aircrew to climb aboard the aircraft if a ladder was not available.

◁ Rear view of the take-off dolly fitted to the Ar 234 V5 showing the outriggers which support the skids beneath the turbojets. As can been seen these were braced by struts fastened to the centre of the mainwheels.

△ An excellent close-up view of the take-off dolly fitted to the Ar 234 V5. This was very similar to that used by the V3 and V4 but had strengthened support struts.

◁ The spring-loaded box mounted behind the main axle of the dolly contained the parachute which was deployed on take-off. This slowed the dolly, preventing it from damage, and even worse, from striking the aircraft as it bounced along the runway.

Take-off dolly
fitted to the Ar 234 V5, V6, V7 and V8

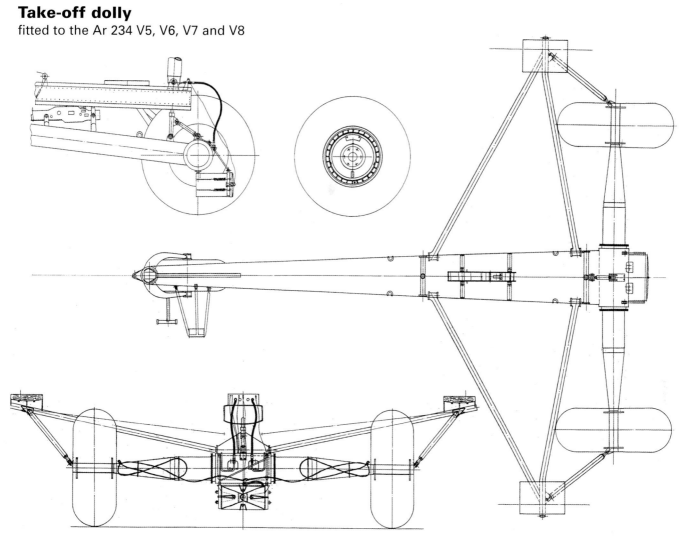

◁ The combined engine nacelle arrangement developed for the Ar 234 V8 was used, in a slightly modified form, for the Ar 234 C-3 production model. Very few of these advanced bomber/reconnaissance aircraft reached the *Luftwaffe* before the end of the war.

Central retractable skid
fitted to the Ar 234 A

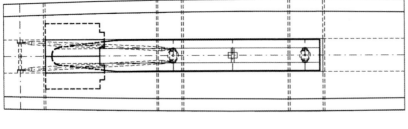

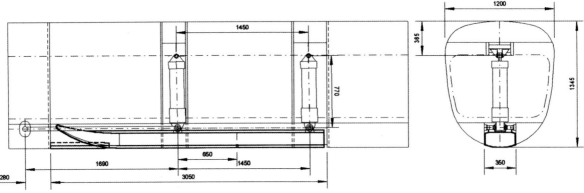

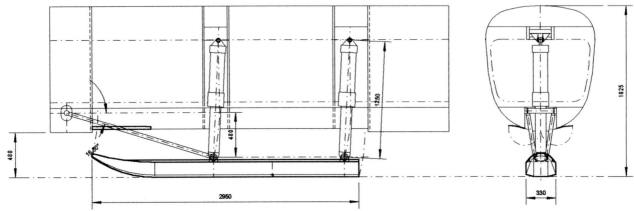

△ Three drawings of the central retractable skid fitted to the Ar 234 A. The top drawing shows the skid viewed from below, the centre a side view with it retracted and the bottom with it extended. Two large hydraulic rams were mounted inside the fuselage which were tilted forward by the small connecting strut when the skid was extended.

◁ A close-up view of the main hydraulically-operated retractable skid mounted below the fuselage of the Ar 234 V1 while it was under construction.

◁▽ The improved dolly and skid arrangement fitted to all Ar 234 A-series prototypes from the V3 onwards. The balancing skids beneath the turbojets, which were extended by a single hydraulic ram, were supported by dolly outriggers during take off.

▽ The photograph bottom left shows the shows the modified skid as fitted to the V1, while the photograph bottom right shows the improved design on the Ar 234 V5 which was also fitted to the V7.

△ A Walter 109-500 rocket engine mounted on a wheeled maintenance dolly. The parachute allowing the engine to return to earth after burn-out and be re-used has still to be fitted to the nose of the unit.

△▷▽ A sequence of stills taken from a cine film showing the Ar 234 V2 taking off with the aid of its two Walter Ri 202 (HWK 109-500) booster rockets. These engines produced 500 kg (1,100 lbs) thrust for 30 seconds and proved vital in assisting the Ar 234 to become airborne when carrying heavy loads.

▷▽▽▽ After completing their 30 second burn period, the Walter rocket engines were jettisoned to fall to the ground with the aid of parachutes mounted in the nose. They could then be collected and re-used.

◁▽ The cockpit interior of the Ar 234 A-series differed considerably from that of the Ar 234 B production model. Rather unusually, the major instruments, including the airspeed indicator, compass, artificial horizon, altimeter and rate of climb indicator were separated and mounted in two consoles forward of, and on either side of the pilot. The twin throttles were to the pilot's left, with the engine instruments to his right. In the later B-series, a new panel was provided above the control column housing the main instruments in a more conventional layout.

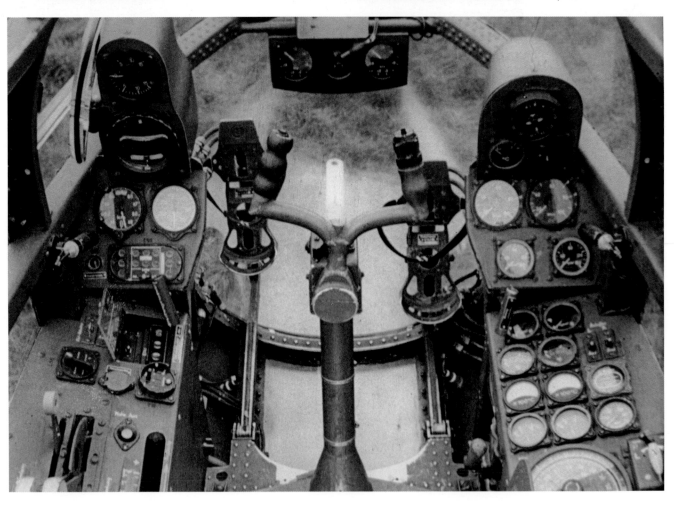

◁ The extensively glazed *Plexiglas* cabin of the Ar 234 V2 showing the open hinged crew entry hatch.

▽ An Arado mechanic runs up the engines of the Ar 234 V2 during a servicing session. Just to the left of the red cross, marking the position of the first aid kit, can be seen the lead plugged into the fuselage side to provide auxiliary power. The white half circles painted on the fuselage sides mark the position of the kick steps.

△▽ Arado test pilot Ubbo Janssen being assisted into the cockpit of the Arado 234 V5 during the spring of 1944. One problem with the aircraft that it was extremely difficult for the pilot to exit the cockpit in the event of an emergency. Proposals were made to equip it with an ejector seat, but such a device was never fitted.

△▷▽ A sequence of photos illustrating the method adopted for starting the BMW 003 engines of the Ar 234 V6. For this, a specially-built dolly was designed on which was mounted a conventional piston engine. This was hitched up to the turbojet and engaged, spinning the compressor to a point where fuel could be injected into the combustion chamber and the engine started.

E 02347020 V6

△◁ The Ar 234 V4 coming in to land at the point of deploying its braking parachute, at Alt Lönnewitz airfield with all three skids extended. This was the last prototype to be powered by pre-production Jumo 004 A-0 turbojets.

△▷ The Ar 234 V3 was first machine to be tested with a braking parachute on 24 February 1944. Further tests followed and were so successful that the device was later fitted to the standard production Ar 234 B-2.

△▷ As Erich Sommer returned from flying the world's first jet reconnaissance operations, he saw that the *Versuchsverband's* Ju 352 transport, T9+AB, had arrived at Juvincourt. These photographs show the ground crews unloading spares from the aircraft with the aid of its '*Trapoklappe*' hinged ramp. To the left of both pictures is a spare take-off dolly while, in the centre, can be seen the oddly-shaped wheeled jacks which were used to lift Ar 234 A-series aircraft back onto their dollys.

△△ Ground crews lift Erich Sommer's Ar 234 V7, T9+MH, back on to its take off dolly with the aid of specially designed wheeled jacks. The whole process took about twenty minutes to complete during which the aircraft was extremely vulnerable to Allied attack.

◁ This photograph of the Ar 234 V1 shows to advantage the hydraulic jacks fully extended and the dolly being carefully put into position prior to lowering the aircraft into its position.

"It was a completely new flying experience"

"It was really wonderful! I was reminded of Galland's words that it felt as thought angels were pushing. It gave such an impression of harmony. The aircraft promised a legendary performance…"

Erich Sommer

Erich Sommer was born on 12 December 1912 in Munich. His first operational unit was KGr 100 which he joined in December 1939 as a navigator. He was awarded the Iron Cross First Class on 24 September for operations in Norway and over the British Isles. After a short period in Africa he was transferred to the Versuchsverband OKL, training as a pilot during the spring of 1944.

Following the decision to test the Ar 234 operationally two pilots from the 1./*Versuchsverband OKL* were made available to fly them.they were *Oblt.* Horst Götz and *Oblt.* Erich Sommer. Sommer had already been treated to a preview of the aircraft in July 1943 when he was asked by *Maj.* Siegfried Knemeyer, on Göring's personal staff, to examine the first prototype at Brandenburg. He remembers his first view of the aircraft, which at that time was propped up on its manufacturing cradle:

"The aircraft only had wooden mock-ups of the real engines, but the shape of the shoulder-wing airframe was sleek with a beautiful finish. I then met some designers, engineers and a director, *Dipl.-Ing.* Wilhelm van Nes. After a lot of explanation by the gentlemen I sat in the pilot's seat to get the feel of it.

"After climbing out I had two main criticisms to put to the gentlemen. Firstly, why was a gliding attack suggested for the bomber? A shrugging of shoulders was the answer. Secondly, that a rear view mirror inside the cabin would not work for the single-man crew because the *Plexiglas* would ice over at high-altitude. In its place I suggested a periscope, similar to that developed for tanks.

"My own answer to the first question was that this new aircraft should use all its high speed and altitude to operate unmolested by fighters. Dive bombing would be inaccurate because the high gliding speed without the braking effect of the propellers would lead the pilot into the flak danger zone and air turbulence of lower altitudes. Conversely, a high-altitude attack could be planned well in advance with the *Lotfe* bombsight controlling the aircraft by the three-axis autopilot. 'Yes', they said, and got excited about the idea."

Horst Götz was the first of the two to actually fly the Ar 234, taking the V5 up for a 30 minute flight during the evening of 1 June 1944. He told the authors in 1985:

"The take-off procedure was not very complicated. First I engaged the starter, then fed petrol into the combustion chamber until, at approximately 6,000 rpm, I made the gradual change to J2 kerosene. The engines were then revved up to their maximum 9,000 revolutions. After take-off I throttled the engines back to cruising speed.

"It was a completely new flying experience. Only a slight whistling noise in the cockpit could be heard. The take-off dolly had functioned quite normally. It was really wonderful! I was reminded of Galland's words that it felt as thought angels were pushing. It gave such an impression of harmony. The aircraft promised a legendary performance, and before long I was speeding over the Elbe and the Rhine before landing back at Alt Lönnewitz on the skids. This felt just like landing a glider."

Four days later Erich Sommer made his first 15 minute flight in the aircraft, echoing the impression that Götz gave previously:

"It was an exhilarating experience to fly nearly vibration free with only the wind noise over the fully glazed cabin and flying fast, even in a throttled back circuit. ...For take-off on the grass strip we had two Walter rockets beneath each wing which were dropped after becoming airborne. The dolly was slowed by a braking parachute which opened automatically the moment the aircraft separated. Likewise the rockets came down on parachutes after their release to be refuelled again... So take-off was a dramatic event with the roaring of jet engines, then the roar of the rockets and smoke and stink and finally peaceful parachutes waving in the air – when they opened, which they often didn't."

Götz flew the V4 on 6 June followed by two more flights in the same prototype by Sommer on the 7th and 8th. Two days [5] later Götz continued another familiarisation flight in the V4 followed by two flights of over an hour on 12 and 15 June in the V5. Both were from Alt Lönnewitz, the second being an experimental reconnaissance flight at altitudes of up to 6,000 m (19,000 ft). It was probably during one of these two flights that Götz had a similar mishap to that suffered earlier by Janssen when the dolly would not release.

"This was a risky business because it just hung there under the release mechanism. The smallest mistake on my part could

Horst Götz

Horst Götz was born on Christmas Day in 1911. He made his first flight on 29 September 1933 in an Udet Flamingo, joining the Luftwaffe from the Telefunken company on 26 August 1939. He served with KGr 100 before joining the Versuchsverband (known as the VfH at that time) in July 1942. Apart from flying the Ar 234, Götz also flew the Ju 86 R and the Ar 240, both over Britain. He died in 2000.

5. According to Götz's logbook, this flight took place on 11 June 1944.

During an early flight in the Ar 234 V5, Horst Götz found that he could not release the take-off dolly. This problem had happened earlier to Ubbo Janssen on 2 April 1944 and he was forced to land with it still attached. This sequence of photos show the aircraft taking off, approaching Alt Lönnewitz airfield and landing with the fuselage main skid under compression. Unfortunately the dolly skids had been disconnected and the V5 careered along the runway out of control. Eventually the aircraft came to a halt in a potato field where it slowly tipped from the dolly. Fortunately only slight damage was caused to the wing tip.

have slammed the dolly into the aircraft which would have been the end of me. While I made few careful turns around the airfield, I requested by radio to clear the airfield in order so that I could come in diagonally in order to use the longest possible landing strip. I knew that the brake hoses had been torn away and that I had no brakes to land this fast bird. My radio message had been acknowledged, but the airfield was not cleared. The man in charge, *Ing.* Arno Trebs, prohibited his men to do that and commented: 'Let him try to land safely as best he can.' Yes, we had characters like him too in those days! I brought the crate down at a great lick and ended up in a potato field. Mother Earth had embraced me again."

When he was told of Trebs' failure to co-operate, the airfield commander was furious. The aircraft itself suffered little damage although its turbojets were so badly clogged with straw that they had to be flushed out with a hosepipe.

Talking to Joachim Carl, production test pilot at Alt Lönnewitz, Sommer was surprised to discover that no high altitude flights in the region of 11,000 m (36,000 ft) and endurance tests of over an hour had been made. When he asked why, Carl replied that: "That is a matter for the *Luftwaffe* test pilots at Rechlin. We company test pilots don't want our flying career shortened by high altitude flying in unpressurized aircraft with the resulting arthritic complaints."

Consequently, Sommer decided to take matters into his own hands. On 26 June 1944 he took the Ar 234 V7 up on an experimental photographic flight lasting an hour and a quarter, climbing to 11,000 m and attaining a speed of 590 km/h (367 mph) in a dive. Three days later he exceeded this feat. He flew three times around a 300 (186 mile) triangle before landing at Alt Lönnewitz, reaching an altitude of 10,000 m (33,000 ft) and covering a distance of 1,435 km (892 miles) in a flight lasting two and a half hours (*see appendix 4*). When he eventually landed, with only ten minutes fuel left in its tanks, the fear of Arado personnel for his safety quickly turned to elation when they realized that their design had slightly *exceeded* the calculated performance submitted to the RLM - a rare occurrence.

Although the two pilots had proved that the V5 (now coded T9+LH) and the V7 (T9+MH) were ready for action no orders were given for their deployment. The reason for the delay seemed inconceivable to the two pilots. Götz, who had been assigned to lead the unit, commented in fury:

"The Allied invasion was running full tilt. I assumed that *Kommando Götz* was moving west and reported our two jets ready for action. I also had a Ju 352 as a transport aircraft. Nothing happened! The traitors in the highest leadership positions did not want the invasion to be interfered with. On 17 July, we finally received permission (not orders) to fly to Juvincourt on the Invasion Front. No airlifting of the technical equipment, but transport by rail which was a very dangerous undertaking in those days. The saboteurs or idiots were at it again. I divided our special equipment onto two freight trains. Only one arrived at the destination."

As Götz said, his *Kommando,* a detachment of the *Versuchsverband*, finally left their home base of Oranienburg

Arado Ar 234 V5/V7
with Jumo 004 B engines
and Walter HWK 109-500
take-off rockets

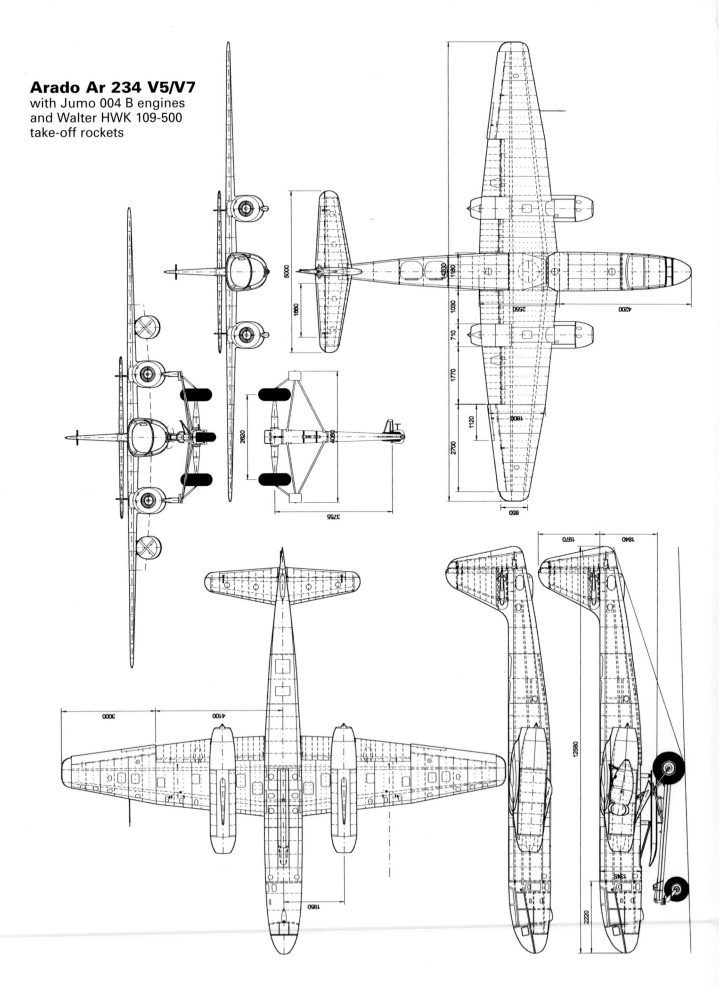

Arado Ar 234 V7, W.Nr. 130007

This aircraft flew the world's first jet reconnaissance sortie on 2 August 1944 piloted by Oblt. Erich Sommer. This revolutionary aircraft was able to operate almost without fear of interception and was at last able to provide German High Command with some idea of Allied activity in Normandy.

north-west of Berlin for Juvincourt near Reims in France on 27 July. Their task was to reconnoitre the beachhead area where the Allies had landed some weeks before. Even the transfer failed to go smoothly, an engine of Götz's aircraft failing, forcing him to return to Oranienburg. Sommer's V7 did reach Juvincourt safely where it was hoisted on to a low-loader and towed into a hangar. Here it was to stay until its take-off dolly and other essential fuel and transport vehicles were delivered by rail. Some of this failed to arrive after it was destroyed in Allied air attacks as Götz had predicted. At this time the *Kommando* had an 18-man *Luftwaffe* ground crew, two airframe experts from Arado and an engine technician from Junkers.

Finally, on the morning of 2 August, Sommer was at last able to prepare his V7 for *Kommando's* first operational sortie, the world's first by a jet-propelled reconnaissance aircraft. After a

△ This photograph was taken by Erich Sommer from the Ar 234 V7 high over the invasion beachhead during the world's first jet reconnaissance sortie on 2 August 1944.

◁ As Erich Sommer returned from carrying out the world's first jet reconnaissance operation he saw below him that both Götz's V5, T9+LH, and the unit's transport Ju 352 A-1, T9+AB, had arrived at Juvincourt. This photo shows the spare take-off dollys and other equipment being unloaded from the Junkers with the aid of the 'Trapoklappe' hinged ramp. To the right of the photograph Sommer can be seen striding away, clutching his 8mm cine camera.

△ Another photo taken from Sommer's V7, this time of Götz's V5 being towed to its dispersal at Juvincourt.

▽ The Ar 234 V5 preparing to take-off from its concrete runway. The big problem with the Ar 234 A-series was that it had to take off on a concrete runway and land on grass. Then followed 20 minutes of vulnerability to aerial attack while it was jacked up and returned to its take-off dolly before it could be moved.

taxiing for about 200 m (650 ft) he fired the machine's two rocket-assisted take-off pods. Within seconds the aircraft was soaring into the air, its boosters trailing smoke. After about half a minute the rockets, their fuel exhausted, were jettisoned and Sommer headed the V7 westward, climbing steadily until he reached an altitude of 10,500 m (35,000 ft). High over the Cherbourg Peninsula he reversed course and put the aircraft into a shallow dive to build up speed to about 740 km/h (460 mph). Levelling off, he concentrated on flying straight and level so that his cameras could faithfully record the scene below. The weather conditions could not have been better, with scarcely a cloud in the sky. His first run covered the strip of coastline where the Allies had landed almost two months before. Then he turned west to cover a strip 10 km (6 miles) further inland and, this completed, he turned east again to make a third run a further 10 km inland. Following this his camera indicators indicated that their film was exhausted and he headed back to his base.

"As I came in for the approach to Juvincourt I saw that our Ju 352 (T9+AB)had landed and that Horst's V5 was nearby being winched up onto its tricycle. Turning on to my final approach I nearly crashed into the ground. With the flaps in the take-off position, the skids lowered and the engines idling, the aircraft wanted to turn turtle in spite of my applying full opposite aileron. I only got her back on an even keel by applying full power and inching the trim forward just above the ground. It was frightening and couldn't be explained. After this we avoided similar flight situations with the power off."

Following his safe landing, the mechanics converged on the aircraft to unload the camera magazines and return the aircraft to its take-off dolly. During this single sortie Sommer had been able to accomplish more than the whole *Luftwaffe* reconnaissance force in the west had managed in two months. It took a team of 12 interpreters two days to produce an initial report from the 380 photographs which he had taken. They revealed that the Western Allies had been able to land one and a half million men and almost a third of a million vehicles in France since D-Day. "After that first sortie," Sommer recorded, "lots of senior officers came to Juvincourt wanting to look at the aircraft, but the whole thing was kept very secret and they were not allowed near it."

In the three weeks that followed, the two aircraft flew a total of seven additional missions, four by Götz and three by Sommer. The last of these, on 26 August, was over Paris which had just fallen to Allied forces. The now inexorable advance eastward by the Allies forced the *Kommando* to leave Juvincourt for Chievres in southern Belgium two days later. Sommer again arrived safely, but as it approached Mons, Götz's V5 was hit by accurate *German* anti-aircraft fire which knocked out its hydraulics.

◁ As Horst Götz was forced to belly land the V5 at Oranienburg after its hydraulics had been damaged by German anti-aircraft fire, the Plexiglas nose shattered and showered him with flying stones. He was temporarily blinded in the crash, forcing him to wear bandages and dark glasses for a few weeks.

"I decided to fly to the Arado factory at Brandenburg for repairs. Upon arrival I noticed that the area had been carpet-bombed and that everything was burning. My fuel tanks were showing empty and the red warning light was on. I decided on impulse to divert to Oranienburg. I barely made it, going for a direct approach without flaps or the benefit of the skid at 300 km/h. Sand and stones hit my face. Like an idiot I had forgotten to put on my safety glasses, which we always carried with us. The aircraft had stopped and had no damage other than the hit received by the anti aircraft fire. I was well except I could not

△◁ After Götz had been helped from the shattered cockpit of the Ar 234 V5 at Oranienburg, its destruction was completed when a taxiing Fw 190 crashed into its rear killing its pilot. This above photograph of the remains shows one of the aircraft's Rb 50/30 cameras in the rear fuselage. The photograph to left shows the damaged wingtip.

△△▷▽ On 1 June 1944 all four BMW 003 A-0 engines of the Ar 234 V6 suffered successive failures after only 17 minutes flying. Ubbo Janssen managed to make a successful belly landing on the Torgau-Eilenburg railway line near Eilenburg, north-east of Leipzig but neither this aircraft or the other four-engined machine, the V8, ever flew again.

see. The corneas of both eyes had some damage. I crawled out of the cockpit and lay down in the grass next to the aircraft. The medical orderlies collected me and I was treated by a doctor."

Shortly afterwards the V5 was completely destroyed when it was rammed from behind by a taxiing Fw 190.

Before Sommer could fly any further operations he was forced to move on to Volkel in Holland on 30 August. Then, four days later, that base was heavily bombed by a force of about 100 RAF Lancasters. After some craters in a taxi track were filled in, Sommer managed to leave Volkel on 5 September, heading for the *Kommando's* new base at Rheine near Osnabrück. The night after their arrival at the base, Sommer's men, about 36 in all, were awoken by a group of soldiers from an infantry unit whose leader flourished an order that they were to hand over their weapons. Furious at this, Sommer went to see the unit's commander who apologised profusely, but explained that he had received an order from "that idiot Himmler" who considered that *Luftwaffe* units retreating from France were a rebellious element ready to mutiny.

Four days later Sommer received orders from *Luftwaffen Kommando West* at Limburg to carry out a reconnaissance sortie over the Thames Estuary. He made this sortie the next day, extending the flight to cover London. During the outward leg, flown at altitude through cloudless skies, he passed an RAF Mosquito travelling in the opposite direction and obviously bent on a similar mission. Both airplanes being unarmed, the pilots could only wave to each other before hurrying on their separate ways.

"Next morning I received a call just before take off for The Wash area of eastern England. Some exalted voice from Limburg HQ informed me that I had exceeded my authority by filming London. A 'high-up' was upset and a 'blood judge' was on his way to court martial me. I immediately telephoned Horst at Oranienburg to see if he could find out who was behind this. Was it Fatso Göring, or Goebbels or Himmler, the latter pair worrying

◁ During their operations from Juvincourt, the Ar 234 reconnaissance Kommando was joined by Kommando Schenck, a jet bomber unit equipped with the Me 262. Here Götz (left) chats with pilots from the unit including Major Wolfgang Schenck (the tall figure in the centre).

▷ Walter Wendt joined the Ar 234 reconnaissance Kommando from the Telefunken electronics company. He made several training flights in the Ar 234 V7 followed by a few operations in an Ar 234 B. He was killed on 25 November 1944 when an engine of a new B-series aircraft (W.Nr.140304), which he was collecting from Oranienburg, failed on take-off.

that my film would blow away their propaganda that their 'Wunderwaffen' were about to bring a victorious end to the war. We didn't trust any of them anymore."

On receiving Sommer's call Götz, who was still recovering from his eye injuries, asked to be driven to Limburg where he threatened to ground the *Kommando* unless the charges were dropped. He then flew back to Berlin where he attempted to arrange a meeting with Josef Goebbels, Hitler's Propaganda Minister, who he thought might be responsible for the charges.

"I did not think much about the risks I was taking. I was fully aware that it was risky for a unit commander to leave his *Staffel* without orders... I marched into the Propaganda Ministry… and was happy to speak to an adjutant…The court martial judges were recalled, charges were dropped and everything returned to normal. My friend was saved and the whole thing was soon forgotten. Long after the war I found out who was our opponent and who had demanded Sommer's and later my head. It was *SS-Obergruppenführer* Hans Kammler, chief of the V-2 programme. This man wanted to prevent any information about the failure of his V-2 programme reaching his *Führer's* ears."

Following Sommer's sortie over The Wash on 11 September he probably completed another four operational flights in the V7 before the *Kommando* began to receive the new, and much improved, Ar 234 B-2 with a conventional retractable undercarriage. This meant that the last operational A-series prototype probably flew no more operational missions, remaining on hand for training. Finally, on 19 October 1944, one of the *Kommando's* new pilots, *Fw.* Walter Wendt had the port engine skid of the aircraft collapse on take-off. He tried to bring it to a halt but this only caused it to fall off its dolly, damaging the fuselage and rudder. After makeshift repairs Götz flew the aircraft to Oranienburg the next day where it was retired from service.

▽ The destruction of the Ar 234 V5 enabled Horst Götz to return to operations with an early Ar 234 B-series aircraft which was fitted with a conventional retractable undercarriage.
This was actually the twelfth production aircraft, W.Nr.140112, coded T9+GH.

Appendices

Appendix One

```
                        R e p o r t

              on the testing of the Ar 234 V1
                                                    S e c r e t !
              during the period 18.7 to 31.7.43.


Sunday,      18.7. Transport of aircraft to Rheine. Re-assembly begun.

Monday,      19.7. Assembly completed.

Tuesday,     20.7. Functional testing of the hydraulics. Elimination of
                   control problems.

Wednesday,   21.7. Static engine testing. Taxiing trials. Jacking up of
                   the aircraft on to the dolly to test the brakes.
                   Simultaneous fitting of the parachute container to
                   the dolly. Further taxiing trials.

Thursday,    22.7. Functional tests: Simulated dolly jettisoning
                   resulted in damage to release cable (a new cable was
                   obtained from Brandenburg). Taxiing trials
                   with rocket assisted take off equipment but without
                   TL (turbojets) followed. Finally taxiing with TL.

Friday,      23.7.)Elimination of minor functional problems. Measuring
                  )and Sunday,
             25.7.)checking of the complete engine measurements
                  )(automatic observation).

Monday,      26.7. Static engine testing to check the regulators;
                   during this the port engine caught fire at over
                   3000 rpm owing to a leak in the injectors. Removal
                   of the engine.

Tuesday,     27.7. Repair of the engine by the Junkers company.

Wednesday,   28.7. Re-fitting the engine. Examination and calibration
                   of instruments for the port engine. Static testing
                   to check the regulators.

Thursday,    29.7. Altering the tailplane trim tabs which were tail
                   heavy. Further testing of release procedure for the
                   take off dolly. Functional tests: Dolly release OK.

Friday,      30.7. Flight No.1, 20.10 - 20.24 hours, 1st factory test
                   flight (without rocket assistance). Destruction of
                   take-off dolly after the parachute caught on the
                   mainwheel support struts.

Saturday,    31.7. General control of the aircraft. Altering of the
                   tailplane trim tabs to be nose heavy (Details: -
                   1.50 to + 1.50).

Brandenburg/Havel, 5.8.43
TAe-Fl Sommermeier/Sche.
```

Transcription by Vorwald of a **General Luftzeugmeister** *conference held on 5 October 1943 regarding the crash of the Ar 234 V2.*

(Reference Milch Document 26, p.7433. Although the date of the crash is reported as 2 October 1943 in the following report, all other documents give the date as the 1st.)

Generalmajor **Wolfgang Vorwald** (Chief of Technical Air Armament):
"The Ar 234 V2 disintegrated and crashed on 2 October, the pilot is dead. He told me that at high altitudes the turbojets tended to malfunction at times. After a flame-out they would fail to restart. Up to 4.5 km (15,000 ft) they were faultless. This flight was carried out at altitude of 9 km. There was radio communication almost to the end. The pilot only realised that there was a catastrophe imminent at the very last moment; up until then radio conversation was quite normal. The tailplane had failed, an engine had stopped working and there was instability around the elevators and ailerons. The pilot tried to restart the engine as he lost altitude. All instruments failed and the pilot must have become disorientated. At an altitude of 500 m (1,600 ft) flames spurted from the aircraft. The presumption is that a fuel line had worked loose and that inflammable material set fire to the wiring, causing instrument failure and control surface malfunction."

Generalfeldmarschall **Erhard Milch** (overall head of the RLM's technical department):
"I have gained a different impression from the report."

Vorwald:
"At the last moment he jettisoned the canopy but failed to bale out. It could be that his attempt to restart the engine caused the fire."

Milch:
"He said that the port engine failed at 9,000 m. He tried to restart it at 4,500 m. Then the aircraft appeared to dive. His last report stated that all instruments had failed and that there was vibration in the elevators and ailerons. If there had been a fire, he would have said so. I am convinced that during the dive he exceeded the speed of sound and this caused the instruments to fail and the airplane to go out of control."

Oberst **Ernst Pasewaldt** (with the RLM's Technical Department):
"I have an impression that there was an internal fire."

Milch:
"I don't see how it could burn. The pilot reported quite calmly and sensibly at 4,500 m that the first thing that had failed was all the instruments. Surely all of them could not have been knocked out by the fire?"

Pasewaldt:
"They are electrically operated. The main leads are situated above the engine. If they burn through, they would short circuit."

Hoffman: (on Pasewaldt's staff)
"At 8,950 m Selle reported that the port engine had failed. He glided down to 4,500 m at a indicated speed of 300 km/h (185 mph) but experienced elevator vibration at this velocity. He then said that he could not extend the landing skids. Shortly afterwards the airspeed indicator failed, and he tried to extend the skids manually. One and a half minutes later he reported vibration in the elevators and ailerons. Through binoculars it was possible to see that the port engine was on fire throughout the whole period of the glide following its failure. The instrument connections, which run via the engines to the wings, must have burned through, causing all flight instruments to fail. The elevator vibration was the result of the nearby push rod being damaged by the fire, and Selle's attempt to lower the skids further aggravated matters."

Milch:
"You were able to ascertain all this from the wreck of the aircraft?"

Hoffman:
"Yes indeed."

Milch:
"Then the report I received is completely false. It states that the aircraft went into a dive at 4,500 m and, further, that all instruments had failed. I cannot explain it otherwise."

Hoffmann:
"The engine detached itself from the aircraft before it hit the ground. This is very interesting because it leads us to conclude that the fire (of which there were overwhelming signs in the engine) had not commenced at 1,500 m but at the altitude at which Selle had attempted to restart the engine."

```
                                              1./Vers Verb O.K.L.
                                                         Secret!

Kommando O.K.L.
Oberltn. Sommer                                  Alt-Lönnewitz,
3.7.1944.
```

F l i g h t   R e p o r t

of 29.6.1944 with the V7

All-up weight with 2 take-off rockets 8,212 kg. Fuel load 3,705 l.

Aircraft was towed, fully fuelled, to take-off point
                    Take-off 11.55

Take-off was normal. Dolly separated only after third strong pull on the manual release lever. The take-off rockets could only be jettisoned after 12 minutes as the electrical release was non functional.

Climb after 12 minutes with n = 8,700 (full power). The climb rate was very slow. Time to 10,300 m was 30 minutes. External temperature at 10,000 m was -340 C. During the last high altitude flight [on 26.6.44] a temperature rise of 60 C by air friction on the thermometer was established. A climbing time of 22 minutes was then achieved at -540 C external temperature. At 8,000 m the 3. Exhaust needle position was reached. The Gas temperature did not rise because of this. (6200/5900). At 12.37 an altitude of 10,000 m was reached. Ground covered during the climb with and against the wind was 225 km. Climb speed was between Va 320/360 km/h in steps so that the speed did not increase. The climbing performance was very unusual. The cause was not clear. Fuel pressure, P7 and gas temperature were quite normal. The landing skids indicator showed 'up'. Fuel flow from the tanks was unequal. Fuel content, at 10,300 m, of the forward tank showed 750 l., the rear 1,180 l.

Level flight at 10,000 m:

Return to 10,000 m. Fuel transfer pump switched on. After 10 minutes the speed increased to Va 425 km/h. Fuel transfer time 38 min. The camera sliding doors were opened for 20 min. After 10 min. throttled back to n = 8,500 and both engines switched to the rear fuel tank. The switch control light went out. Medium readings were then:

Va = 425 km/h, P7 = 0.5/0.5 n = 8,500/8,500
Fuel pressure 11/10, gas temperature = 610/590.

For weather reasons a course between Magdeburg and Ruhrland was selected as there was 5/10 cloud cover enabling a back and forth path. The flight characteristics of the aircraft were normal, with the exception of a slight dropping of the starboard wing. The extended trimming range was sufficient to compensate. The trimming ratchet got stuck occasionally but was released by more forceful action.

Location above ground and time were continually registered, as well as times required for turns at turning points. A rear view mirror fixed in a temporary position inside the top of the cabin was only useful during ascent but proved useless at altitude as the cabin roof panes iced over. All other cabin panes in the field of vision stayed ice free. My own lengthy condensation trail (as observed from the ground) was not visible to me.

At 13.53 and above the airfield, a fuel reserve of 750/500 l, i.e. 1,200 l was recorded. The flight was programmed to end with a fuel reserve of 1,200 l.

Descent:
During descent both engines were run constantly at 10 ata and at a continuously corrected speed of over 700 km/h. The course covered was airfield – Dessau – airfield, a total of 170 km. Instrument readings were taken at an altitude of 8,000 m 6,000 m, 4,000 m and 2,000 m. When, at 500 m

Continued overleaf

in horizontal flight, the rear fuel tank suddenly indicated 350 l, both engines were switched to the forward tank.

At 14.10, that is after 17 mins descent and over the airfield, the engines were fully throttled back and another fuel reading was taken, with 600/350, that is a total of 950 l. The aircraft landed after a 270 degree turn of 5 min at 14.15; a total flying time of 140 minutes. After measurement by stick on the ground it was found the remaining fuel was 300/150 l (450 l total) whereas the indicators showed 300/100 l. The oxygen pressure, after 110 min high altitude flight, fell from 160 atü to 90 atü. 100% oxygen 'showers' were used frequently. The cameras were, after the fitting of oil deflectors, smoothing of sharp angles by puttying and the fitting of felt strips inside the fuselage, completely free of traces of oil.

Evaluation

Take-off to beginning of climb
Flying time	12	min
Fuel consumption at n = 8,000	450	l
" 1/h per turbojet	1,100	1/h
Distance flown at Va 300 km/h	60	km

Climb to 10,000 m
Time	30	min
Fuel consumption under full power	1,000	l
" 1/h per turbojet	1,000	1/h
Distance flown during climb	220	km

Horizontal flight at 10,000 m
Time	76	min
Fuel consumption	1,420	l
" 1/h per turbojet	560	1/h
Distance flown	950	km
Calculated true speed	760	km/h

Descent throttled back to 10 ata
Time	17	min
Fuel consumption	320	l
" 1/h per turbojet	560	1/h
Distance flown	170	km
Landing not including a 5 min circuit	5	min
Fuel consumption	180	l
Distance flown	30	km

Totals
Flying time	140	min
Fuel consumption	3,270	l
Distance flown without landing	1,405	km
Fuel reserve	450	l

Ar 234 V1

TG+KB   **W.Nr.130001**   **Port engine: Jumo 004 A-016**
                                  Stbd. engine: Jumo 004 A-06

Flight	Date	From	To	Time	Pilot	Notes	Place
						Report concerning the pre-flight testing of the Ar 234 V1 from 18 Jul 43 to 31 Jul 43 at Rheine.	–
	30 Jul 43	–	–	–	Kröger	Pilot plus three Arado personnel and guests arrived at Rheine in the Ar 232 A-08 (W.Nr.0010) to witness the first flight of the Ar 234. They returned on 31 Jul 43.	–
1	30 Jul 43	20.10	20.24	14 min	Selle	Dolly destroyed after release when the parachute became entangled in the support struts at the rear. (Two parachute containers were mounted directly in front of the supports that held the dolly's mainwheels).	Rheine
	06 Aug 43	–	–	–	Kröger	Flew with Hans Rebeski in an Ar 96 (W.Nr.3733) to Rheine with modified support struts for the parachute containers which enabled them to be moved further forward.	–
	07 Aug 43	–	–	–		Problems during ground testing with the port engine. This was replaced with W.Nr.1003000038 originally intended for the V3 which had been almost completed at Brandenburg. Report on the testing of the V1 between 1 Aug and 11 Aug 43.	–
	10 Aug 43	–	–	–	Kröger	Pilot plus three Arado personnel and guests (including Hans Rebeski) arrived at Rheine in the Ar 232 A-02 to observe the second flight of the V2. Returned on 11 Aug 43	–
2	10 Aug 43	16.37	17.31	54 min	Selle	Second dolly destroyed when its parachute again caught on the mainwheel support struts (previously ferried from Brandenburg by Kröger and Rebeski in an Ar 96). Following this it was decided to release the dolly immediately after take-off.	Rheine
	28 Aug 43	–	–	–	Kröger	Flew with Peter in an Ar 79 (W.Nr.0060) from Brandenburg to Rheine to observe the third flight of the V1. Returned on 29 Aug 43.	–
3	29 Aug 43	16.56	17.14	18 min	Selle	Take-off dolly modified so that a single parachute container was mounted *behind and below* the mainwheel support struts. With this new arrangement the dolly was released just after take-off at about 150 km/h (90 mph) and it deployed without problem. Prototype made an emergency landing on the outskirts of Rheine airfield following problems with the engines. It was badly damaged and never flew again.	Rheine

The V1 completed a total of three flights totalling 1 hr 26 min

Ar 234 V2

DP+AW		W.Nr.130002		Port engine: Jumo 004 A W.Nr.1003000040 Stbd. engine: Jumo 004 A W.Nr.1003000035		
Flight	Date	From	To	Time	Pilot	Notes	Place

Flight	Date	From	To	Time	Pilot	Notes	Place
1	13 Sep 43	10.42	11.30	48 min	Selle	First take-off with the aircraft transferring from Brandenburg to Alt Lönnewitz. Equipped with the first type of dolly with the third braking parachute arrangement.	Brandenburg to Alt Lönnewitz
2	14 Sep 43	16.10	16.48	38 min	Selle	Engine measurement tests.	Alt Lönnewitz
3	16 Sep 43	15.55	16.18	23 min	Selle	Engine measurement tests.	Alt Lönnewitz
4	23 Sep 43	10.08	10.48	40 min	Selle	Engine measurement tests.	Alt Lönnewitz
5	01 Oct 43	15.03	15.43	40 min	Selle	Engine measurement tests. The aircraft crashed following a fire in the port engine which resulted in the death of the pilot. The report of 19 Oct 43 which followed called for the installation of automatic fire extinguishing equipment in the V3 and ejector seats in the V3, V4, V5, V8, V9, V10, V11, V15, V16 and V17.	Alt Lönnewitz
	01 Oct 43					Report of Selle's death in the V2.	
	01 Oct 43				Kröger	Flew with guests (including Rebeski) in the Ar 232 A-05 (W.Nr.0007) to Alt Lönnewitz following Selle's crash.	

The V2 completed a total of five flights totalling 3 hrs 09 min

Ar 234 V3

DP+AX		W.Nr.130003		Port engine: Jumo 004 A W.Nr.1003000037 Stbd. engine: Jumo 004 A W.Nr.1003000028		
Flight	Date	From	To	Time	Pilot	Notes	Place

Flight	Date	From	To	Time	Pilot	Notes	Place
1	29 Sep 43	18.12	18.33	21 min	Selle	New design of take-off dolly with outriggers to support the turbojet skids. The first involved the transfer of the aircraft from Brandenburg to Alt Lönnewitz. Possibly used rocket assisted take-off equipment.	Brandenburg to Alt Lönnewitz
2	30 Sep 43	15.27	15.57	30 min	Selle	Take-off dolly released at 2 metres altitude but was damaged.	Alt Lönnewitz
3	11 Nov 43	11.12	11.29	17 min	Kröger	First flight after Selle's death.	Alt Lönnewitz
4	12 Nov 43	09.30	10.17	47 min	Janssen	First flight with Janssen at the controls, starboard engine problems, forcelanded at Jüterbog-Damm.	Alt Lönnewitz to Jüterbog-Damm
5	15 Nov 43	14.52	15.05	13 min	Janssen	Return flight from Jüterbog to Alt Lönnewitz.	Jüterbog-Damm to Alt Lönnewitz
	(26 Nov 43)	–	–	–	–	On 21 Nov 43 the V3 was transported by road to Insterburg where it was shown to Hitler on 26 Nov 43. Returned by road.	

Ar 234 V3 continued

Flight	Date	From	To	Time	Pilot	Notes	Place
6	18 Dec 43	10.38	10.50	12 min	Janssen	Experiments with ice skids with teeth, snow depth of between 3 and 6 cm, considerable reduction in landing speed was attained.	Alt Lönnewitz
7	24 Jan 44	11.20	11.40	20 min	Janssen	Hydraulics test.	Alt Lönnewitz
8	28 Jan 44	11.10	11.30	20 min	Janssen	General test (This flight seems to have been confused by Janssen with the 4th flight of the Ar 234 V5).	Alt Lönnewitz
9	28 Jan 44	16.05	16.25	20 min	Janssen	General test.	Alt Lönnewitz
10	04 Feb 44	14.21	14.37	16 min	Janssen	General test.	Alt Lönnewitz
11	05 Feb 44	11.15	11.30	15 min	Janssen	General test.	Alt Lönnewitz
12	22 Feb 44	11.07	11.17	10 min	Janssen	Braking parachute package attached and tested in flight. Main skid collapsed on landing but little damage suffered.	Alt Lönnewitz
13	24 Feb 44	13.39	13.44	5 min	Janssen	First flight test of braking parachute.	Alt Lönnewitz
14	25 Feb 44	13.13	13.18	5 min	Janssen	Second flight test of braking parachute.	Alt Lönnewitz
15	28 Feb 44	15.38	15.56	18 min	Janssen	In an attempt to solve the problem with the skids, Hans Rebeski suggested that they be raised and lowered twice before landing to ensure hydraulic pressure was at its maximum. This was successfully tested on this flight.	Alt Lönnewitz
	03 Apr 44	–	–	–	Kröger	Take-off aborted because of seized brakes.	Alt Lönnewitz
16	05 Apr 44	08.05	08.17	12 min	Kröger	Take-off dolly would not release, this was caused by a failure of the electrical system in flight, landing had to be made with the dolly attached.	Alt Lönnewitz
17	13 Apr 44	16.07	16.38	31 min	Kröger	Control force measurements.	Alt Lönnewitz
18	27 Apr 44	11.45	12.11	26 min	Janssen	Functional flight for control force measurements in co-operation with the Askania company.	Alt Lönnewitz
19	30 Apr 44	09.50	10.36	46 min	Grube	General test, flight quality excellent, skid collapsed on landing, supports twisted.	Alt Lönnewitz
20	11 May 44	14.57	15.36	39 min	Janssen	Control force measurements.	Alt Lönnewitz
21	13 May 44	10.11	11.02	51 min	anssen	Control force measurements.	Alt Lönnewitz
22	01 Jul 44	12.18	13.06	48 min	Janssen	Control force measurements.	Alt Lönnewitz
23	06 Jul 44	17.45	18.23	38min	Janssen	Control force measurements.	Alt Lönnewitz
24	07 Jul 44	19.48	20.36	48 min	Janssen	Control force measurements, probably no further testing as aircraft was now considered "obsolete", being replaced by the Ar 234 B-series.	Alt Lönnewitz

The V3 completed 24 flights

Ar 234 V4

DP+AY **W.Nr.130004** **Port engine: Jumo 004 A W.Nr.1003000031**
Stbd. engine: Jumo 004 A W.Nr.1003000036

Flight	Date	From	To	Time	Pilot	Notes	Place
1	26 Nov 43	12.21	12.40	19 min	Janssen	Equipped with rocket-assisted take-off units, problems with the port engine during taxiing.	Alt Lönnewitz
2	06 Jan 44	09.40	10.20	30 min	Janssen		Alt Lönnewitz
3	08 Jan 44	08.52	09.51	59 min	Janssen		Alt Lönnewitz
4	11 Jan 44	13.30	14.15	45 min	Janssen		Alt Lönnewitz
5	20 Jan 44	10.32	10.55	23 min	Janssen	Transfer flight from Alt Lönnewitz to Brandenburg for a demonstration before Milch and Saur.	Alt Lönnewitz to Brandenburg
6	21 Jan 44	14.25	14.50	25 min	Janssen	Demonstration flight at Brandenburg and return to Alt Lönnewitz.	Brandenburg to Alt Lönnewitz
(7)	28 Jan 44	09.40	10.00	20 min	Janssen		Alt Lönnewitz
(8)	06 Feb 44	13.23	14.05	42 min	Janssen		Alt Lönnewitz
(9)							Alt Lönnewitz
10	22 Feb 44	15.45	16.34	49 min	Kröger	Test of landing flaps up to 60 degrees.	Alt Lönnewitz
11	07 Mar 44	14.07	14.24	17 min	Janssen	Demonstration, landing flaps not fully extended.	Alt Lönnewitz
12	15 Mar 44	16.23	16.32	9 min	Kröger	Split flap tests, the landing flaps were not fully extended on landing.	Alt Lönnewitz
13	16 Mar 44	16.19	16.27	8 min	Kröger	Split flap tests, the landing flaps were not fully extended on landing.	Alt Lönnewitz
14	30 Mar 44	–	–	7 min	Kröger	Split flap tests.	Alt Lönnewitz
15	02 Apr 44	11.34	12.16	42 min	Kröger	Split flap rudder tests, and landing flaps extended to 53 degrees, fuel had to be transferred from the port tank to the starboard engine.	Alt Lönnewitz
16	05 Apr 44	10.48	11.26	38 min	Kröger	Split flap rudder tests, and landing flaps extended to 53 degrees, fuel had again to be transferred from the port tank to the starboard engine. Aircraft needs repair.	Alt Lönnewitz
17	07 Apr 44	15.38	16.00	22 min	Janssen	Transfer flight from Alt Lönnewitz to Brandenburg. Several detailed improvements required. Aircraft could be improved by reference to Rechlin.	Alt Lönnewitz to Brandenburg
18	31 May 44	20.45	21.15	30 min	Janssen	Transfer flight from Brandenburg to Alt Lönnewitz.	Brandenburg to Alt Lönnewitz
19	05 Jun 44	16.45	17.00	15 min	Sommer	Familiarisation flight, rocket assisted take-off from Alt Lönnewitz, Sommer's first jet flight. Experiments with instrument flying.	Alt Lönnewitz
20	06 Jun 44	11.15	11.30	15 min	Götz	Familiarisation flight. Times given in Arado report. According to Götz's logbook, this flight was a 30 minute flight between 10.30 and 11.00.	Alt Lönnewitz
21	07 Jun 44	11.37	12.10	33 min	Sommer	Familiarisation flight.	Alt Lönnewitz
22	08 Jun 44	15.12	15.55	43 min	Sommer	Familiarisation flight.	Alt Lönnewitz
23	09 Jun 44	11.14	11.32	8 min	Janssen	Demonstration to the General der Truppentechnik, main skid did not extend properly.	Alt Lönnewitz
24	10 Jun 44	10.04	10.25	11 min	Götz	Familiarisation flight. Times and date given in Arado report. According to Götz's logbook, this was a 30 min flight between 11.00 and 11.30 and took place on 11 Jun 44.	Alt Lönnewitz
25	15 Jun 44				Sommer	Possible additional training flight, aircraft was put into reserve.	Alt Lönnewitz

The V4 completed at least 24 flights

Ar 234 V5

GK+IV	W.Nr.130005 T9+LH	Port engine: Jumo 004 B W.Nr.1003000030	Stbd. engine: Jumo 004 B W.Nr.1003000023

Flight	Date	From	To	Time	Pilot	Notes	Place
1	22 Dec 43	12.25	12.45	20 min	Janssen	Take-off with rocket assistance from the factory at Alt Lönnewitz. Janssen could not reduce speed to idling and had to drop the aircraft on to the concrete runway causing the skids to collapse which damaged the wingtips and port wing. Pilot had a good impression of the V5's flight characteristics.	Alt Lönnewitz
2	20 Jan 44	–	–	25 min	Janssen	General test flight after repair.	Alt Lönnewitz
3	27 Jan 44	16.05	16.12	7 min	Janssen	General test flight.	Alt Lönnewitz
4	28 Jan 44	11.10	11.30	20 min	Janssen	General test flight. (In his logbook, Kröger claims to have made this flight on 20 Jan 44, a 25 min flight number 3804. He incorrectly quotes the *Stammkennzeichen* as GK+IF).	Alt Lönnewitz
5	09 Feb 44	–	–	21 min	Knemeyer	Familiarisation flight, further flights to be made.	Alt Lönnewitz
6	22 Feb 44	15.22	15.45	23 min	Janssen	Vibration experienced in the starboard wing due to a panel coming loose near to the engine. First flight with snow skis which caught in ruts on landing resulting in their collapse and the shattering of the cockpit glazing. Skid unsuitable.	Alt Lönnewitz
7	06 Mar 44	15.04	15.47	23 min	Janssen	Flight performance.	Alt Lönnewitz
8	02 Apr 44	14.16	14.35	19 min	Janssen	Flight performance. The dolly would not release after take-off and the pilot was forced to land with it still attached. He disconnected the brakes on the dolly, but this caused the aircraft to overshoot and run into a field. The right skid connection failed tipping the aircraft off the dolly and causing slight damage to the underside of the fuselage.	Alt Lönnewitz
9	07 Apr 44	15.43	16.09	26 min	Kröger	Dolly braking parachute failed, dolly crashed into woods.	Alt Lönnewitz
10	12 Apr 44	17.07	18.00	53 min	Janssen	Instrumentation measurements in association with Zeiss Ikon at Dresden.	Alt Lönnewitz
11	13 Apr 44	18.05	19.03	58 min	Janssen	Instrumentation measurements in association with Zeiss Ikon at Dresden, bad weather.	Alt Lönnewitz
12	20 Apr 44	09.34	10.14	40 min	Janssen	Instrumentation measurements, problems with radio equipment, the port skid failed on landing and the aircraft slewed around.	Alt Lönnewitz
13	24 Apr 44	15.10	16.25	1 hr 15 min		Eheim Instrumentation measurements in association with Zeiss Ikon at Dresden.	Alt Lönnewitz
14	10 May 44	11.28	11.48	20 min	Eheim	Instrumentation measurements in association with Zeiss Ikon at Dresden. Electro-mechanical failure of dolly release, finally jettisoned at 300 m (1,000 ft) but was destroyed despite braking parachute deploying. On landing the hydraulics failed in both main and outrigger skids and the aircraft was slightly damaged.	Alt Lönnewitz
–	–	–	–	–	–	Fitted with two Rb 50/30 cameras in the rear fuselage.	
15	01 Jun 44	13.24	13.36	12 min	Janssen	Factory test flight, aircraft handed over to 1./*Versuchsverband OKL* as T9+LH.	Alt Lönnewitz
16	01 Jun 44	17.00	17.30	30 min	Götz	Familiarisation flight. Pilot's overall impression was very enthusiastic.	Alt Lönnewitz
17	12 Jun 44	15.00	16.15	1 hr 15 min	Götz	Familiarisation flight.	Alt Lönnewitz
18	15 Jun 44	16.14	17.25	1 hr 11 min	Götz	Photographic flight up to 6,000 m (19,000 ft).	Alt Lönnewitz

Ar 234 V5 continued overleaf

Ar 234 V5 continued

Flight	Date	From	To	Time	Pilot	Notes	Place
19	7 Jul 44	07.05	07.36	31 min	Götz	Transfer flight, aircraft now re-coded T9+LH.	Alt Lönnewitz to Oranienburg
20	7 Jul 44	13.39	14.05	26 min	Götz	Familiarisation flight.	Oranienburg
21	11 Jul 44	14.17	15.27	1 hr 10 min	Götz	Familiarisation flight.	Oranienburg
22	02 Aug 44	14.57	17.20	1 hr 23 min	Götz	Transfer flight.	Oranienburg to Juvincourt
23	8 Aug 44	18.10	19.39	1 hr 29 min	Götz	Operational sortie over St.Malo.	Juvincourt
24	11 Aug 44	14.32	15.30	58 min	Götz	Operational sortie over Armentieres.	Juvincourt
25	–	–	–	–	Götz	According to Götz's memory he flew another operational sortie around this time although it is not recorded in his logbook.	Juvincourt
26	25 Aug 44	10.25	11.30	1 hr 5 min	Götz	Operational sortie.	Juvincourt
27	28 Aug 44	10.35	11.34	59 min	Götz	Hit by German flak near Brussels during a transfer from Juvincourt to Chievres. The aircraft's hydraulics were damaged so Götz made for Brandenburg where repairs could be carried out. Heard that the airfield was burning from an Allied attack and diverted to Oranienburg where he made a belly landing. Cockpit glazing smashed, pilot temporarily blinded. Aircraft was later hit by a taxiing Fw 190 which completed its destruction.	Juvincourt to Oranienburg

The V5 probably completed 27 flights

Ar 234 V6

GK+IW	W.Nr.130006	Port engines	(inner) W.Nr.386286, (outer) 386289
		Starboard engines	(inner) W.Nr.386288, (outer) 386236

Flight	Date	From	To	Time	Pilot	Notes	Place
1	25 Apr 44	14.32	14.56	24 min	Janssen	First flight. To be used in comparison flights with the Ar 234 V8 which made its first flight on 04 Feb 44.	Alt Lönnewitz
2	27 Apr 44	15.00	15.41	41 min	Janssen	Flight characteristics and engine tests.	Alt Lönnewitz
3	30 Apr 44	08.14	08.52	38 min	Janssen	Engine test.	Alt Lönnewitz
4	12 May 44	18.13	18.42	29 min	Janssen	Engine test, problems with fuel feed to all engines from the tanks.	Alt Lönnewitz
5	17 May 44	18.58	19.31	33 min	Janssen	Engine test, problems with fuel feed to all engines from the tanks.	Alt Lönnewitz
6	30 May 44	17.19	17.55	36 min	Janssen	Problem-solving flight, engine test.	Alt Lönnewitz
7	01 Jun 44	18.45	19.02	17 min	Janssen	Emergency landing on the Torgau-Eilenburg railway (6km NNW of Eilenburg) following the failure of all four engines. Good landing but aircraft subsequently damaged by fire in engine which was still running.	Alt Lönnewitz

The V6 completed a total of seven flights totalling 3 hrs 38 min

Ar 234 V7

GK+IX
T9+MH

W.Nr.130007

Engines: Jumo 004 B
Engines: Jumo 004 B

Flight	Date	From	To	Time	Pilot	Notes	Place
1	22 Jun 44	09.55	10.25	30 min	Kröger	First flight, fitted with two Rb 50/30 cameras in the rear fuselage, aft skid support strut collapsed due to hydraulic fault.	Brandenburg to Alt Lönnewitz
2	26 Jun 44	11.25	12.40	1 hr 15 min	Sommer	Photographic flight to 11,000 m (36,000 ft) a speed of 950 km/h (590 mph) attained in a dive, no complaints.	Alt Lönnewitz
3	29 Jun 44	11.55	14.25	2 hr 30 min	Sommer	Range and photographic flight, height of 10,000 m (33,000 ft) and distance of 1,650 lm (1,025 mls) achieved, triangular flight via Magdeburg, no complaints. *See Appendix 3.*	Alt Lönnewitz
4	08 Jul 44	–	–	–	Sommer	Transfer flight.	Alt Lönnewitz to Oranienburg
5	25 Jul 44	15.00	16.41	1 hr 41 min	Sommer	Transfer flight.	Oranienburg to Juvincourt
6	02 Aug 44	–	–	–	Sommer	First operational flight over the invasion beachhead.	Juvincourt
7	06 Aug 44	–	–	–	Sommer	Second operational sortie over the Cherbourg area.	Juvincourt
8	11 Aug 44	–	–	–	Sommer	Third operational sortie over the Cherbourg area.	Juvincourt
9	26 Aug 44	–	–	–	Sommer	Fourth operational sortie over Paris.	Juvincourt
10	28 Aug 44	–	–	–	Sommer	Transfer flight to Belgium in the face of the Allied advance.	Juvincourt to Chievres
11	30 Aug 44	–	–	–	Sommer	Transfer flight to Holland in the face of the Allied advance.	Chievres to Volkel
12	5 Sep 44	–	–	–	Sommer	Transfer flight to Germany in the face of the Allied advance.	Volkel to Rheine
13	10 Sep 44	–	–	–	Sommer	Operational sortie over the Thames Estuary and London, encountered a Mosquito over the North Sea.	Rheine
14	11 Sep 44	–	–	–	Sommer	Operational sortie over The Wash area	Rheine
	–	–	–	–	Sommer	Götz, still at Oranienburg, reports that 14 operational flights had been made with the Ar 234 V5 and V7. As he made 4 flights with the V5 and six had already been made by Sommer, four more were probably made by Sommer in the V7.	
	8 Oct 44	–	–	16 min	Götz	Familiarisation flight.	Rheine
	12 Oct 44	–	–	20 min	Götz	Familiarisation flight.	Rheine
	19 Oct 44	–	–	–	Wendt	Wendt had the port engine skid collapse on takeoff. He tried to bring it to a halt but this only caused it to fall off the dolly, damaging the fuselage and rudder.	Rheine
	19 Oct 44	11.00	11.53	53 min	Götz	After makeshift repairs Götz flew the aircraft back to Oranienburg where it was retired from service.	Rheine to Oranienburg

Ar 234 V8

GK+IY		W.Nr.130008		Port engines Starboard engines		(inner) W.Nr.386244, (outer) 386241, (inner) W.Nr.386243, (outer) 386239	

Flight	Date	From	To	Time	Pilot	Notes	Place
1	04 Feb 44	16.15	16.26	11 min	Janssen	The world's first four-jet aircraft to fly. Difficulties with engines, split flaps for high speed flight questionable.	Alt Lönnewitz
2	04 Mar 44	11.00	11.22	22 min	Janssen	Problems with troublesome fuel distribution to all four engines, landing flaps did not deploy.	Alt Lönnewitz
3	08 Mar 44	17.01	17.27	26 min	Janssen	(Janssen's logbook gives time of flight between 15.20 and 15.46).	Alt Lönnewitz
4	30 Mar 44	14.11	14.41	30 min	Janssen	Two engines failed. (V8 fitted with the hydraulic equipment designed for the V9).	Alt Lönnewitz
5	17 Apr 44	16.05	16.35	30 min	Janssen	Electrical failure caused take-off dolly to jam, finally released at 500 m (1,600 ft) but destroyed.	Alt Lönnewitz
6	06 May 44	13.40	14.08	28 min	Janssen	Further problems with transfer of fuel to all four engines.	Alt Lönnewitz

The V8 completed a total of six flights totalling 2 hrs 27 min